The Map of Rumania

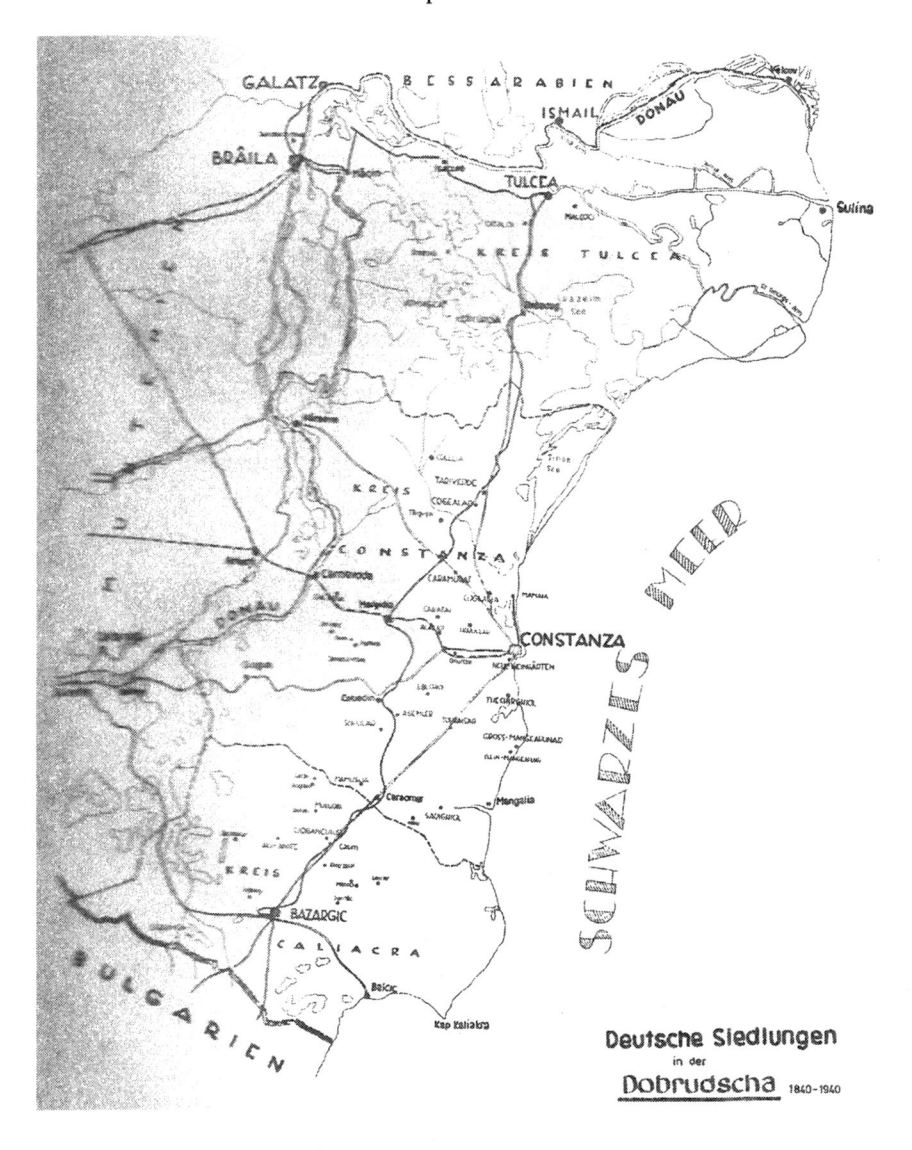

Deutsche Siedlungen
in der
Dobrudscha 1840-1940

Maria, Gypsy Princess

Memories of A German Girl through and After World War II

Maria Reule Woelfl

iUniverse, Inc.
New York Bloomington

Maria, Gypsy Princess

Copyright © 2009 by Maria Reule Woelfl

All rights reserved. No part of this book may be used or reproduced by any means, graphic, electronic, or mechanical, including photocopying, recording, taping or by any information storage retrieval system without the written permission of the publisher except in the case of brief quotations embodied in critical articles and reviews.

The views expressed in this work are solely those of the author and do not necessarily reflect the views of the publisher, and the publisher hereby disclaims any responsibility for them.

iUniverse books may be ordered through booksellers or by contacting:

iUniverse
1663 Liberty Drive
Bloomington, IN 47403
www.iuniverse.com
1-800-Authors (1-800-288-4677)

Because of the dynamic nature of the Internet, any Web addresses or links contained in this book may have changed since publication and may no longer be valid.

ISBN: 978-1-4401-6739-3 (sc)
ISBN: 978-1-4401-6740-9 (ebk)

Printed in the United States of America

iUniverse rev. date: 01/18/2010

Acknowledgment

I am grateful to my family, especially my husband, Bob. Without them this story would not be told. I Frau Irmgard Gerlinde Stiller and her son Wolfgang Stiller who gave me permission to use photographs of people who lived in Bessarabia at the time my family did. I am grateful to all who donated photographs for this book, including my sisters and my nieces. Also my granddaughters Dawn and Amanda thank you for your help in putting the finishing touches to the story. Most of the photos came from the cookbook, Die Kuche der bobrudschadeutschen Bauerin 1840-1940. (From the Kitchen of the Bobrudscha-German farm women) Author Irmgard Gerlinde Stiller –Leyer.

Foreword

The order came from Hitler himself. We were to leave our homes in Rumania and move to his occupied territories. We were to bring only what we could load on wagons, drive fifty kilometers to the Danube River and board a ship for Austria. All Germans living outside the Führer's Third Reich were ordered back. For our "loyalty" we would be given homes, farms and or businesses of those who had fled the Nazi invaders. The Fuhrer's orders were to be carried out to the letter. . .

It was 1940. I was five-years-old and understood only that my parents, grandparents and sisters, as well as my aunts, uncles and cousins were being uprooted from the only home we had ever known. Our ancestors had left Germany and migrated to Rumania in the 1800s to escape a famine. Wars and revolutions, with kings and Kaisers fighting for power while peasants worked and starved to feed their armies, who were forbidden even to hunt game on the huge estates of the declining aristocracy. Women and children were left to till and harvest fields as the men were conscripted as soldiers, nothing new in does days. That is why many poor and hungry German families wandered to different countries to make new lives for themselves. Our forefathers came from an area near Stuttgart Germany. Mostly farmers with close-knit families and a few tradesmen thrown in all worked together for the common good.

Now, a hundred years later, their descendants were being ordered back to the German territories. Thirty-seven families left the small Romanian village of Alakap that fall. Other German families living in Bessarabia did the same. Those who were ill left the previous spring. Our mother, who had tuberculosis, was among them. She and many others were taken to sanitariums or hospitals in Austria not far from the town of Graz.

We were displaced people now.

****

Maria Reule Woelfl

When I was a child, I saw through the eyes of a child. I pictured myself a free spirit with clear thoughts and wanderlust in my heart. When I was older I remembered things differently then my sisters and I told them so. I believed certain events happened when I was child, but they often shook their heads and said, "Oh, Mariechen, it didn't happen that way at all."

My usual response was, "But it did. You just saw it differently." I knew it was so. When I told them, I remembered stomping grapes with my feet when I was four.

They said, "No, no, that was sauerkraut, not grapes."

I answered, "I remember having purple feet afterward."

They still disagreed.

I said, "I knew the barrel I urinated into at age four years old was grapes, not sauerkraut. I knew it made the wine even sweeter."

They'd shake their heads, and we would all laugh. I always insisted I was a princess and not born into the Reule clan. My sister, Vickie, remembered it differently. She said when she was five years old she awoke in the middle of the night with an earache, and Papa come to comfort her. He told her not to cry because she had a new baby sister. She also said that I looked like them, so I had to be a Reule. I still felt I was a princess, born to royalty. Maybe I was a princess in my former life!

I also believed, and still do, that I was born into that certain time and family because I needed to learn certain lessons, to advance spiritually and reach a higher level of awareness. All my life, I felt I was being tested to see how well I would perform in this world of upheaval. These experiences were challenging, and I have grown to be a stronger person because of it. I thank God for the lessons.

Life is precious and there is good in the hearts of all people. In God's eyes there is only one color and that color is love.

Mama and Papa

Chapter 1
Alakap 1939-1940

My great grandparents, Heinrich and Christine Reule, migrated to Rumania in the early 1800s. About twenty families started their own villages, including the town of Kobadin where my grandparents settled.
It was barren land with nothing but dust and hardly any water. With only picks and shovels and wheelbarrows to carry the dirt away, it took years to dig wells.

My mother's family lived in Musalia near Constanta on the Black Sea where the elite went to play. My mother and father met in Kobadin and were married there. Later they moved to Alakap where Victoria and I were born.

When we left Alakap in the fall of 1940 the German settlement had grown considerably. My grandparents, Caroline Nee Broneske and Jakob Reule, had eight children, as did most families. Grandpa and grandma Reule had four boys and four girls. My father, Gottlieb, was in the middle, so he was elected to help his mother fetch and carry and do the things around the house for her. He hated it because everyone called him the "Kuchen Miechel" (kitchen-yokel), a demeaning job. One good thing he would say that came out of it was that he enjoyed good food and learned how to cook; witch became very useful later in life.

Maria Reule Woelfl

Reule Family

By the time I was born most of my father's brothers and sisters were married too and had a lot of children. My aunt and uncle, Paulina and Edward Schultes, lived next to us with their six children. My aunt and uncles Emile Hopp lived on the other side of us, and Uncle Daniel lived across the street, but they left for Germany the year before in 1939. Our grandparents Jakob and Karoline Reule lived in the middle of the next street. A stone wall separated our home from the Schultes'. The houses had yards that where walled on all sides, each with a huge gate that was closed at night. The wall between Schultes' yard and ours had fallen down years before. No one thought to rebuild it because it was convenient to cross from one yard to the other. My cousin Edmund was my age, and we were inseparable. Two blondes that looked so much alike, people thought we were twins. We played together and walked barefoot, hand-in-hand all over the village. Most people knew us and just smiled when they saw us wander.

Each household had several guard dogs chained during the day and let loose at night. Edmund and I were scared of those dogs. They'd chase us barking, but they couldn't reach us. The clanging chain and snarling unnerved us, so we ran as fast as we could and often stumbled and fell head long in the muddy streets. We just picked ourselves up and kept on, mud all over our faces, while the dogs fought to get loose, almost choking themselves.

Another animal that scared us even more was the gander. If we got too close to a baby gosling, the gander went crazy, hissing and flapping his big wings, chasing us all over the yard as we ran, screaming for our mamas. The

Maria, Gypsy Princess

gander wouldn't give up. He chased us until someone came to our rescue. We had a lot of these escapades. Now I realize how wonderful our life was, innocent and carefree. It didn't last nearly long enough.

The Schultes family

****

The Gottlieb Reule clan consisted of papa, mama, Amelia, and their seven girls: Anna, Emma, Gottliebe, Ida, Alma, Victoria and Maria, (Mariechen as they all called me). I was the youngest, pampered and taken care of. My father, although he had hoped the seventh would be a boy, still doted on me, as did my mother and sisters.

Life was no bed of roses for the Reules, though. The whole family worked hard. All of my sisters had their chores to tend to, helping mama in the house and also milking the cows and feeding the animals. My three older sisters also worked for our father in his vegetable and flower business. He was a Gemusehandler; they grew every vegetable you can imagine, ripened on the vine and very tasty. They were freshly picked and sold at the market or shipped to big cities to sell. It was a family concern, but father also had other people working for him, mostly women, except the overseer, who was a man. Vickie was always stuck watching me, which she didn't like one bit.

She would whine, "Mama, do I have to? Can't Alma do it?"

"You know Alma has her own chores," my mother would respond.

When Mama wasn't looking, Alma would stick out her tongue at Vickie and run outside. Vickie tried to tell, but Mama held up her hand, "Enough! Take Mariechen outside with you, and be sure to watch her."

We also had livestock, horses, cows, sheep, chickens, geese, ducks and even doves. Father would go out and shoot jackrabbits sometimes, and mama made delicious rabbit stew. "Hasen Pfeffer," it's called in German.

Behind the barn was a small orchard with all kinds of fruit trees. Mama and the older girls canned fruit and vegetables every fall. What a chore that was. There was a small building in the yard we called the summer kitchen, also an oven built of clay bricks. Mother baked bread once a week in that oven big, delicious golden loaves so yummy with thick slices and were smeared with homemade butter and preserves, makes my mouth water even now.

"Green" was a way of life for my family. We recycled and lived organically way before anyone used those words. I should say that, in today's world of global warming when our planet itself is threatened, if we want a guide to going "green," all we have to do is look to our past. The land gave us all our food. We made our own clothes. We did no damage to the earth. Our transportation was horse drawn wagons and our own feet. We had candles and kerosene lamps, and the animals gave us fuel for cooking, as you will see. Of course, few people can live like this in today's modern world, but there is a lesson in knowing it was possible, and not so long ago.

We churned our own butter, and of course buttermilk was good to drink afterwards. Cottage cheese was made from sour milk, and Mama made Kuchen with the cheese. Then the liquid was used for making the bread dough. Our stove was made of the same bricks and had an iron plate on top with small round holes. When the plate was removed food cooked faster. They canned all the fruit, meats and vegetables in that summer kitchen. Next to the house was a cooling shed where we stored canned goods and fresh produce. It kept everything fresh. The shed was built of stone that kept the temperature the same summer or winter. Part of the shed's floor was sandy soil where the root vegetables were buried to stay fresh and edible all winter.

Everything was homemade. Raw cucumbers were put in barrels or jars, then they were covered with cold well water and spices, salt, fresh dill and garlic. Tight lids were put on, and they were to let stand a few months until they were sour and crisp. We lived off the land and always had clothes to wear and plenty to eat. We didn't have running water, electricity or plumbing in the house, but used kerosene lamps or candles. We used the outhouse during the day and a chamber pot at night. An outside stove was convenient for heating water to wash clothes. We made our own soap, made out of lard, used a washboard then hung the clothes on lines to dry. White thing were laid on the grass and we drew some water on it during the day for the sun to bleach it out. The sun always did it job.

The only things we had to buy were sugar, coffee, cloth and thread to sew with. Mama and my older sisters made all our clothes. Father or one of our uncles took a horse and wagon to Constanta to buy bolts of cloth and with the same material make dresses for us cousins, all about the same age. We looked even more like sisters.

In late spring, after the lambs were born, the shearing started. The baby lambs were really cute! It always amazed me how fast they could stand on their spindly legs and bah, bah, and then waddle to their mothers to feed. It was beautiful to see. After shearing, the wool was washed then laid in the sun to dry. It was stretched and combed, then spun into yarn.

Spinning

Maria Reule Woelfl

The ladies of the village got together once a week in one of their homes to spin wool. They set spinning wheels in a circle in the family room and sat and spun for hours. While spinning they ate sunflowers seeds, cracking them between their teeth and spitting the shells on the floor. When they finished for the day, piles of shells were swept up and thrown in the stove to burn. At four in the afternoon they gathered their belongings and headed home to prepare the evening meal.

After the wool was spun it was tied in different colors and woven into unique and beautiful patterns for warm blankets and beautiful tapestries to hang on walls. They knit sweaters, stockings, socks, scarves, caps, and mittens. We all learned to spin and knit when we were very young.

Baking Bread

Women had a hard life in Rumania rearing six or eight children, cooking, baking, washing, and also feeding and milking the animals. I remember when I was three or four, Mama going out to milk the cows. I followed with a small tin cup from a hook behind the barn door. I held it under the cow and would Mama milked right into my cup. The milk was still warm and really good. The foam gave me a mustache. My sisters would laugh and say, "There goes Mariechen with her milk smile again."

My sister, Gottliebe, would put her arm around me with a delightful grin and wipe the foam off my upper lip with her sleeve. "Mariechen," she'd say, what is there to be done with you?" I'd put my arms around her and answer, "Du solst mich nur libe habe," which in English is, "just love me."

Maria, Gypsy Princess

She would run her hand through my hair and send me on my way. Then she would go help Mama with the milking.

Hens were set on eggs for hatching, but first we had to take each egg and shine a light through it to make sure the eggs were good. Some hens would sit on the eggs when they weren't supposed to. We shoo them off the nests, and at times they got possessive and would peck our hands as we tried to take the eggs from under them.

The floors in the house where made of clay and had to be smeared over with new clay every week. Two of my sisters did that job. The goop they used was made of clay dirt, water and straw. They folded an old rag to kneel on, then scooped the stuff in their hands, smeared it on the floor and flattened it out with a trowel. They worked from one side to the other, ending by the door. They did one room at the time because it had to dry before we could walk on it.

Everyone had a job, and we worked from dawn to dusk, sometimes even into the night. In the fall there were pigs to slaughter witch was always a huge job. After a pig was caught, its legs were tied, and father would stick a long knife in its throat. If you have never heard a pig squeal, I can tell you its most horrible sound you would ever hear. Someone held a bucket under the gash to catch the blood to make blood sausage. The whole pig was utilized. After the blood was drawn, the carcass was put in a trough full of boiling water to loosen the short prickly hair, then it was taken out and scraped until all the hair was gone.

Bulgarien: Schlachttag in Bardarski-Geran

Pig Slaughtering

Maria Reule Woelfl

It was hung by its hind legs, cut open from top to bottom, and all the intestines were taken out. It was quartered and divided into different parts. Some of the meat was ground for sausage stuffing. The hindquarters were hung in the smokehouse to cure into ham and bacon. The head meat was used for headcheese. Intestines were turned inside out, cleaned, scraped and washed with cold water over and over then stuffed with sausage meat. Fat was rendered to lard, and the skin was fried in grease and became cracklings, called Krieben, our father's favorite snack. We all liked to nibble them. It took days to render down the whole pig, and all the families in the village helped. As soon as the wheat was golden everyone would be at work to cut the wheat, and then came the threshing. The straw was put in piles and hall into the yards to use in the winter for the animals. Grapes were picked, stomped, and father made his own wine and Schnapps. Kraut was put in barrels with cold water, salt, and spices added, then it was stomped down with our feet. A big stone was used to hold it down, and it was stored in the cooling shed until the cabbage turned sour.

Although the weekdays were toiling, life was not all work without any play. On Sunday we all went to the Evangelical- Lutheran church. That is, if the traveling pastor was in the village. Pastor Meyer baptized all of us, and my older sisters were confirmed by him, too. When the minister could not come to our village, an elder would read from the Bible or the New Testament. Older teens taught Bible classes to the young children.

The young people would all pile into a wagon and go to other towns for parties and dances, my sisters were among them and they have a lot of fun. The older people had their parties too, and everyone was invited. When we were very young we learned to waltz and dance the polka. Some of my cousins played instruments as well. It was always festive and fun for the old and young. The young unmarried ladies belonged to a club called the Ferein, a German word for club. At their meetings they all wore the same outfit, in German Eine Trache. The uniform was a white blouse with short puffy sleeves and a jumper over it. The top was black velvet and the bottom light blue. Over that they wore a pale blue apron. They took dancing and singing classes, and after they learned a special dance or song, they would entertain us. I learned to dance when I was four years old.

Older girls learned to cook and bake simple delicious food. Sunday dinner was mostly stewed chicken. Mama would kill an old hen by cutting its head off. The bird would flip flap all over the yard until it bled out. The intestines were taken out and the chicken was cut into pieces then put on the stove and it simmer for hours. When the chicken was tender mama added vegetables and homemade noodles to the broth and it was very tasty. Mama divided the chicken between the seven of us. Father always got the lion's

Maria, Gypsy Princess

share, the legs and a thigh. The rest of the chicken was divided according to age; the other thigh went to mama. Then she gave everyone a small piece of white meat. We all got our special piece. I would always get the wings, someone would get the upper back and the lower back went to someone else. The liver, gizzard, heart, neck and even the feet were divided. There was always plenty of delicious homemade bread, and a wonderful dessert was served after the meal.

Hopp family

I remember the adults gave a big party in the spring of 1940 before our mother and the other sick people left Rumania. All our relatives and some friends from the village were invited. They used the schoolhouse because there were too many guests to fit into one house. Older girls looked after the little kids. That particular evening about ten of us cousins stayed at aunt Sofia's house. My sisters, Alma, Victoria and two cousins, Erma and Erika, were to look after us. I must say that "looking after us" is an exaggeration because when the girls got together they turned wild. We would run through the house from one room to the other, up and down on chairs, tables and beds, then back again.

The dust stirred up so thick it was almost impossible to see from one room to the other. Remember, the floors were made of clay. After we wore ourselves out, we slowed down and opened all the windows to let the dust out. Then the older girls changed the babies, fed them and put them to bed. They also gave the older kids snacks. After they closed the windows again, we sat around the table and they told ghost stories and we played quieter games. One time, we were all relaxing around the table telling stories, when we heard chains clanging and the windows rattling and a sound like the wind howling. The little ones started whimpering, and the older girls giggled. But when it didn't stop, they too were spooked. "Oh, it's only the boys pulling pranks to scare us," they said. But when it got louder and louder we all hid. Some crawled under the bed, others hid in closets and under the table. I don't remember how long we stayed hidden, but some younger kids fell asleep, including me. The older girls finally found enough courage to go outside and discovered that it was the boys scaring us after all, not ghosts.

We were all superstitious and believed in ghosts and goblins. Few would walk near a cemetery after dark. Even in the daytime we go out of our way not to get close to the graveyard. Also everyone wore black for a whole year if someone in the family died. Another old practice I didn't care for was the open casket. I never wanted to look at the dead when they were laid out.

Mama and Grandfather Hopp

My mother, Amelia, was warm and kind hearted and had a beautiful soul. It was amazing the way she always helped and cared for others when they were sick or in need. She worked tirelessly from early morning into the night. With all her own work she still made time to tend and care for sick people in our extended family.

Mama had high check bones and the bluest blue eyes and raven black hair. None of us girls had her coloring. She was beautiful inside and out. All of us girls had hazel eyes like our father. Emma, Victoria and Gottliebe's hair color came closest to our mother's while the other four had lighter brown hair.

Mother took care of one of our aunts and her daughter who had tuberculosis, and that's when our mother was infected with the illness. Of course, it is very contagious and ran rampant in the 19th century. My aunt died in 1939 and her daughter died a year later.

Alma, Ida and Vickie went to school at seven in the morning, while father and the older girls went to work in the garden. Father always came home for the noon meal that was our dinner. Father's stomach was set by the clock, and exactly at noon he would walk into the kitchen, wash his hands and sit at the head of table and say, "Amelia let's eat." His stomach was never off, and he told time by the sun.

Erma, Anna and Emma

The older sisters stayed and ate with the other workers. In the garden was a kitchen equipped with a stove, table and chairs, and they took turns cooking the meals. They put a big cast-iron pot on a hook and cooked stew or borscht in it. Lamb or pork ribs and all kinds of vegetables simmered in the kettle all morning. They took turns stoking the fire and adding fuel to keep it going. Our fuel was dried dung. Cow droppings and straw were gathered from under the animals then scattered in an area of the yard, pounded flat and left to dry. Later it was cut into squares and stored in a dry place. We also used corncobs for fuel. When burned down, the hot coals were put into an iron to press clothes.

Fuel making for burning

The way we watered the vegetable garden was also unique. The well, more like a big hole in the ground, went straight down on one side, and the other side tapered so you could walk down to water level. On the higher end was a wheel with buckets on hooks. The buckets poured water into a trench that narrowed and separated into the furrows. The wheel was operated by a donkey, walking in circles. That's how the plants and flowers were watered morning and evening.

After the noon meal our father took a nap. He got up so early he needed it. Again father had a built in clock. He awoke exactly one hour later and went back to work. Mama also took a half-hour rest. From her rocking chair in the corner of the kitchen she called me to come to her. She lifted me onto her lap, rocking and humming a melody. I was fast asleep in minutes. The younger girls washed the dishes and did their homework. Then they could go play with friends for a while.

We spoke German at home, a Schwabisch dialect. All the German children went to a Rumanian and German school so they could learn both languages. That was the life for the Bodrudscha Germans living in Bessarabia.

Chapter 2
Sisters' Reunions

In 1988 we had a sister reunion at Alma's home in Austria something we had done every two years since 1968. We would meet at a different sister's home, always in Europe. I had made a sentimental journey back to visit all my sisters in five different countries I hadn't seen some of them for over twenty years. My sister Vickie lived in England, Gottliebe in West Germany, Alma, in Austria, Anna in Rumania and Emma in East Germany. I flew to each country and visited each sister for one week. The trip to each sister's Country would make a story of its own.

Sitting around Alma's table in 1988, we were reminiscing about our younger years in Alakap when Vickie excitedly said, "Alma, do you remember when we were little and Maria was a baby, and mama asked us to look after her?"

"Oh my, yes," Alma said, "what a great story. Maria, you'll enjoy this. It's about you and our sow."

Frieda, the Sow and Baby Maria

Eight year-old Alma and five-year-old Vickie were supposed to take care of the baby. Our big family always had dinner at noontime, and there were always eight around the table, my six sisters, mama and papa. I was still a baby then. That day Mama and papa were talking about our sow, Frieda.

"Amelia," Father said to Mama, you better keep an eye on the sow remember, she had a hard time with her last litter and ate some of her piglets. If I hadn't come into the barn in the nick of time she would've eaten them all. She swallowed two before I could stop her."

"Ja I know," said Mama, "I'll try my best to keep an eye on her, but I can't be with her every minute. Hopefully you'll be home when her time comes."

All the girls were silent. Vickie whispered to Alma, "Frieda wouldn't really eat her babies would she?"

Alma just shrugged. "I don't know. She might!"

After dinner papa went to take his nap as he always did. Mama rested too. Alma and Vickie headed for the door.

"Where are you going?" Mama asked.

"Oh, we're just taking table scraps to the sow and then we're heading to Erma and Martha's house to play with dolls."

"All right," Mama said, but I want you to stay with Maria while I do some weeding so be back in a half hour."

The two begged. "Mama, can't Ida watch her?"

"Ida has her own chores so hush and do as I say. You can go play after Maria wakes from her nap. I don't want to hear another word out of either of you."

Grumbling, the girls left for the barn where Frieda was happily lying on her straw bed, grunting. When Frieda heard the girls come in, she raised her head, peeked at them with half-closed eyes, and then lazily put her head back down. Vickie tickled Frieda under the chin. "How are you feeling, Frieda," she said. "You must promise not to have your babies unless mama or papa is around to help."

Frieda grunted noisily, slowly waddled to the trough and munched happily on her scraps.

The girls ran back to the house shouting, "Mama, Mama, Frieda wants to go out and play in her mud puddle. Can we let her out, Mama?"

Mother hushed them. "Shy, I just got Maria to sleep. I'll let Frieda out on the way to the garden. Alma," she added, "sent Vickie to get me when Mariechen wakes up, and stay with her until I come. You understand?"

"Yes Mama," they both said. Amelia went to the barn to let the sow out, then took a stick, tapped her gently on the rump and guided her into the yard. Frieda headed straight for the mud puddle, dug herself a deep hole, rolled around in the muck, happily settling in for a snooze in the sun. In the house, Alma and Vickie watched Maria sleeping peacefully in her cradle.

"Come on," Alma said, "let's go out and play with our friends for awhile.

Vickie was worried. "But mama told us not to leave Maria alone."

"Oh, don't worry," Alma said, "we'll be back before she wakes up."

So off they went.

Reading the sun, Mama wondered why Vickie hadn't come to get her. It's getting late, she thought. I'd better go see what's going on with those girls. On the way, she noticed Frieda had moved to a shady place behind the barn, contentedly sleeping.

Mama walked into the house, wondering why it was so quiet. The girls were nowhere in sight. They had left Mariechen alone. I was wide awake, happily kicking my feet in the air, trying to catch the sun's rays in my little hands. Mama changed and breast fed me and took me with her. She laid me on a blanket under a tree and went back to work.

An hour or so later Alma realized they had stayed away too long?

"Oh my, Vickie, we forgot Maria! Mama is really going to be angry with us."

They took off running as fast as their legs could carry them. When they got to the house they saw the cradle was empty. They searched, but Maria was nowhere to be found. They shrieked in panic.

"Oh God," Alma whined, "What have we done, Victoria? What have we done? Maria is gone, she's really gone."

"I'll bet that sow came and got her," said Vickie. "What if Frieda ate our baby sister? You heard Papa. That sow ate her babies."

Their panic even greater, they raced for the garden, crying and yelling.

"Mama, mama, we can't find Maria. We looked everywhere, but she's gone. We think the sow ate her."

Mama looked at them sternly and shook her finger, trying to keep a straight face. "Quiet down, you're making no sense. And what are you doing here? Why isn't one of you watching your little sister? Alma, I told you to stay with Maria. Tell me what happened."

Alma and Vickie were so frightened they were stuttering and hanging onto Mama's waist, Vickie on one side and Alma on the other, crying uncontrollably.

"Come on out with it, where is Maria?"

"Mama, we're sorry. We just went out for a few minutes and when we came back Maria wasn't in her cradle. We lost her. We think Frieda came in and ate her. Please forgive us, Mama. We love Maria. We didn't mean to hurt her. If we find her we'll never leave her alone again. Never, Mama," they cried. "We promise."

Mama felt sorry for them. She knew they had learned their lesson. She knelt and put her arms around them. "Don't cry anymore. Maria is right over there lying under the apple tree. She's okay."

Their faces lit up. Tears disappeared as they ran to me, grateful I wasn't eaten. They hugged and kissed me, almost squashing me to death in the process.

Frieda had her babies early the next morning. Her birthing was easier this time; the whole family was there to watch the piglets being born, including me. Frieda didn't eat a single one.

Chapter 3

So many memories flow through my mind at the same time. In 1990 we had another sister's reunion at Gottliebes home in Germany. We were sitting around the dining room table reminiscing about the early years in Rumania and Yugoslavia. That's when I brought up for the hundredth time that I was of royal blood and not a Reule.

"Why do you think so?" they all asked again.

"I was stolen by Gypsies from the palace," I said. "They put me in a basket, carried me to our house and set me on the Reule's doorstep. That's where Papa found me and took me to Mama. That's why Mama was always so kind to the Gypsies."

There was silence in the room. They all looked at me and started to laugh, shaking their heads.

Vickie spoke up. "Mariechen, you can deny it all you want, but you're definitely a Reule. I remember the night you were born. "I awoke in the middle of that night crying because I had an earache. Papa came out of his bedroom to comfort me. He sat me on his lap and asked why I was crying, and I told him my ear hurt. He hugged me close and hushed me. Papa told me not to cry, because I had a new baby sister, born just a few minutes ago. 'So you'd better be quiet or you'll wake her up and she'll cry too,' he said. Papa put something in my ear and I felt better. Then he hummed a lullaby, and I went to sleep."

She went on. "So there. You are our sister, after all. In the morning there you were lying in your cradle all bundled up with your eyes closed, your face red and wrinkled like prune. I took one look at you and fell in love instantly."

"I don't care," I said, "I still think I'm a princess. So please treat me as a royal personage."

After that statement we all laughed, and they said in unison, "Yes, your royal majesty." They bowed in mock respect.

Maria Reule Woelfl

Our Last Christmas in Rumania

The holiday season was always exciting. Christmas of 1939 Mama, although sick, was still in the thick of things. Now she mostly supervised and delegated work to my older sisters. Baking and cooking was done ahead of time. Mama could still do most of it herself, but the cleaning was left to my sisters. Mama had already made most of our Christmas gifts. The few still to be finished, Gottliebe and Ida did for her. Our oldest sisters, Anna and Emma, were already married and lived away from home. Anna, her husband and two-year-old daughter, Maria, named after me, lived in Constanta. They were coming for dinner Christmas Day.

Anna and Johan's Wedding

Excitement was in the air as we all took part in holiday preparations. From the ovens came amazing aromas that flowed through the whole house, the fresh baked goods we loved so much. All the families in the area began the holiday baking and cooking in November, even before Advent, and it went on through Christmas and New Year's.

I was the lucky one. I didn't go to school yet, so I was at home to sample all the goodies as soon as they came from the oven. A day or so before Advent, Father brought some evergreen branches and made them into a wreath. The wreath was wrapped with red ribbons, and four real candles were fastened to it. Then it was hung from the ceiling. We lit one candle each Sunday before Christmas.

The German settlers in Rumania celebrated Christmas Eve in a unique way.

In 1939 I was four. I awoke before dawn while it was still dark outside. The silvery moon hung low over the sleeping village. It shone through the small window onto the bed my sister, Victoria, and I shared. Butterflies dancing in my stomach, I could not keep still any longer. I sat up and shook Vickie's shoulder.

"Vickie, Vickie, wake up. Don't you know what day this is?"

Vickie grumbled and turned over. "Go away, Mariechen, let me sleep."

"What's the matter with Vickie? I thought, doesn't she know Kristkind is coming tonight." Kristkind is the Christ Child in German.) I crawled over Vickie, scrambled to the floor, ran and stood on my tiptoes to reach the doorknob. Then I ran to the kitchen. Mama was up fixing breakfast. She would listen to me.

Mama turned with a surprised look. "What are you doing up so early, Mariechen? She turned back, put coffee grounds in the pot and set it on the stove. Come here liebling," she said, lifting me. (liebling means loved one.) She sat in her rocker and put me on her lap. "Now, tell me what you're doing up at six o'clock in the morning?"

Shifting so I could see her face, I said, "Mama don't you know what day this is?"

"Why yes, liebling, it is Christmas Eve day and you should be in bed, otherwise you will be too tired when Kristkind comes tonight with your presents." She pulled me closer, wrapped her big apron around my bare feet and sang a lullaby. "Schlaf Kindlein Schlaf dein Vater hut die Schaf deine Mutter hut die Lamerlein, Schlaf mien Kindlein Schlaf nur ein." Soon I was fast asleep.

It was our tradition to celebrate Christmas on Christmas Eve. Instead of Santa leaving gifts during the night, Kristkind delivered presents in the evening. At four o'clock on Christmas Eve, our family went to church, as did most German families in the village. When we walked into the church we were awestruck by a twenty-foot pine tree brilliantly lit with hundreds of real candles. It was truly a sight to behold. Under the tree were gifts for each child, toys carved from wood, wagons, animals, dogs, horses and rabbits. Dolls were made from left over materials, sewn together and stuffed with wool. Their hair was made of yarn and their eyes were buttons. For the older boys and girls there were hand knitted socks, scarves, mittens and caps. After the services everyone hurried home to wait for Kristkind.

Maria Reule Woelfl

The unique way of celebrating came much later in the evening. Village teenagers, dressed in ancient biblical costumes, went to each German household to re-enact the birth of Christ pageant.

All bundled up in horse hair blankets, we arrived home from church in a sleigh drawn by our horse, Samuel. Mama hustled us into the kitchen while Papa took care of the horse and sleigh. Inside sixteen-year-old Gottliebe, the oldest sister, helped Mama in the kitchen. Alma and Ida took charged getting us undressed and ready for supper.

In the front room candles shone on the Christmas tree. Mama set a splendid table with a white linen cloth, napkins, her best china and silverware. Hanging from the ceiling above was the wreath with four Advent candles glowing. The meal had been prepared before we went to church. Now it only needed to be warmed up. Mama and my older sisters had been cooking and baking for days to make this evening special.

The food was simple but abundant with all kinds of home baked goodies, such as Kuchen, Stolen, Pfeffernussen, Apfelstrudel and assorted cookies, also meat and cheese stuffed pastries. There was steaming hot chicken noodle soup with big pieces of chicken in each bowl fresh home baked bread and butter.

Mama looked around in the front room to see if all was to her liking then nodded in satisfaction. In the meantime, Gottliebe had her hands full trying to keep us four girls under control. We were impatient to get to the front room to see the Christmas tree. When I was a child we never saw the decorated and lit Christmas tree until Christmas Eve after we came home from church. It would be standing in a dark room with the candles lit when we walked into the room and we were awe stuck when we first saw it.

Finally Mama returned, opened the kitchen door and was almost knocked over by Vickie and me trying to run past her into the front room.

"Hold it! Not so fast," she said, catching us both and holding fast. "We will go into supper as soon as your father comes from the stable."

Just then the front door flew open and there was Father.

"Boy, its cold out there!" He blew out the lantern, set it on the floor, and hung his coat on a hook. "What's going on here?" he said. "Why are you all standing in the kitchen doorway?" Not waiting for an answer, he added, "Amelia, I'm starved, let's eat."

"Come," Mama said, and we noisily followed her in. Then all five of us stopped. "Low and behold, there it stood in all its brilliance and splendor, the most beautiful Christmas tree I had ever seen." We were in awe, real candles flickered in the dark room making soft hissing noises and silver tinsel shimmered in the glow. The tree was covered with home made decorations, cookies in all shapes and sizes, walnuts and small animals painted gold, all dangling from silver strings. Chains of colored paper were draped around the

Maria, Gypsy Princess

branches. Silky strands of angel hair looked as if they were spun by a spider working his magic all day and night to finish just in time. On the very top an angel sat dressed all in white with golden hair and a halo suspended over her head.

"I know the tree is beautiful," Papa said, "but we'd better eat. Kristkind won't appear until we finish."

He didn't have to say another word. We all hurried to our chairs, Papa at the head of the table. "Amelia," he said, "lights some lamps so we can see what we're eating."

Mama handed matches to Gottliebe and Ida to light the lamps on the wall.

Our mother seated herself at the other end, bowed her head and folded her hands. "Alma, you may say grace."

There was happy chatter all through out dinner, and as soon as the dishes were cleared and the lamps blown out, we gathered around the Christmas tree and sang carols "O Tannen Baum, O Tannen Baum and Stiele Nacht, Heilige Nacht."

When the songfest ended, Mariechen and Vickie piped up,

"When is Kristkind coming Mama?"

"Any moment now," she replied.

As if on cue, there was a knock on the door. Mama went to answer Victoria and I right behind her. "No, No!" Mama motioned us back. "Wait here." She closed the dining room door behind her. Papa tried to keep Vickie and me quiet, but we were too excited. It seemed Mama was gone forever, but it was only a few minutes. When she came back she sat close to the tree and put me on her lap. Vickie, Alma and Ida stood near, Gottliebe next to Papa. A hush came over the room, all eyes fixed on the door waiting for the drama to unfold.

First three shepherds entered wearing long ancient Hebrew robes, cloths tied on their heads with a band. In their right hands they carried long staffs as they walked slowly into the room, heads bowed in silent reverence. When they came to a small manger set up near the Christmas tree, they knelt to pray.

We watched in great interest as the door opened again and an angel entered. She was wearing a beautiful, blue gown with a silver sash, and on her back were wings fastened crisscross with silver strands. Her blue eyes sparkled in the candlelight, and on her long blond hair was a wreath woven with silver ribbons. She held an olive branch. She walked slowly around the room waving the branch of peace, and announcing the birth of Christ. "Don't be afraid! Behold, Christ our Savior is born unto you this day in Bethlehem."

Maria Reule Woelfl

Kristkind came in next. As the door opened, I couldn't contain myself any longer. I wiggled down from my mother's lap and took off like a shot towards the door. Mama was too fast for me. She caught me by my dress and pulled me back, whispered," Stay by my side, and I will introduce you to Kristkind."

Kristkind was the most beautiful girl you could ever imagine. Her long blond hair hung around her shoulders, and she was dressed all in white with a lace veil and crown of gold on her lovely head. She looked just like a princess in a fairy tale. She carried a basket with beautiful wrapped packages. She smiled and walked to our family, stopping a few feet in front of us.

Mama stood, took my hand and walked to Kristkind. "This is Mariechen, Kristkind. She has a verse to recite for you." With that Mama returned to her seat. With wide shiny eyes, I stood gazing at Kristkind, a finger on my lower lip, not knowing what to do next.

Kristkind bent and put her hand on my head. "Have you been a good girl, Mariechen?"

I nodded shyly.

"I am waiting for you to recite for me," she said.

I glanced back at my mother for moral support. She motioned for me to kneel and recite my verse.

When I finished, Kristkind said, "That was beautiful, Mariechen! Let's see if I can find a package with your name on it in here." She handed me a present.

I turned, ready to run off, but Mama shook her head to indicate I had forgotten something. I immediately turned back, curtsied and thanked Kristkind, then ran to my father. "Papa, Papa! Look! Open it, for me. Will you, Papa? Will you?"

My father picked me up and carried me to the corner where my bed stood. "Liebling," he said, "quiet down. It's your sisters' turn to get their presents now." With that, he sat and put me next to him. "Let's see what you have here." He opened the package. A beautiful new doll! Victoria went to receive her gift from Kristkind. Then Alma, Ida and Gottliebe received theirs according to their age. Gottliebe being the oldest was last. Then Kristkind and the little troop of visitors bid us farewell and a "Frohe Weihnachten" (Merry Christmas), as they walked to the door. Papa gave them shiny new coins and walked them to the door. The troop would make other stops before returning to their own homes for their Christmas. When Papa came back he left the door ajar. He came to the bed where Vickie and I were playing with our dolls, and sat next to us.

Suddenly the door burst open and the most frightening looking beast rushed in, Krambus. He wore an ugly mask and a long stringy horsehair wig,

Maria, Gypsy Princess

scary a monster to be reckoned with. Tied around his waist was a chain that clanged when he moved, and in his hand was a switch to be used on naughty boys and girls. When the three oldest girls saw him, they took off running and screaming, looking for a hiding place. Vickie and I, still on the bed with our father, scrambled behind his back and hung on for dear life. Two pair of frightened eyes peeking out too scared to make a sound. Poor Gottliebe, being oldest, was getting the brunt of the switch.

Father watched the proceedings, rather amused by it all, but when he saw tears in Gottliebe's eyes, he shouted, "Halt, that's enough." The chase stopped immediately. All three girls ran to Mama for protection.

"Now, now, girls, don't cry," Mama said, "you aren't really hurt. See, Papa is escorting Krambus out." Papa took him to the kitchen, filled two glasses of Schnapps, handed one to Krambus and made a toast, wishing each other a "Frohe Weihnachten," Then Krambus left.

Mama went to join Papa in the kitchen. All eyes were on them when they returned. "Don't worry," Papa said, "he's gone." There was a sigh of relief and a jubilant cry from all five of us. Mama carried a tray of refreshments from the kitchen, cookies, candies, hot milk with honey apple cider and a bottle of wine. Gottliebe brought cups and glasses. After we had our refreshments, things got a little out of hand with everyone talking at the same time.

"Girls, please, quiet down," Papa said, "one at a time. Mariechen, since you are the youngest, you go first. Come, show us what Kristkind brought you, and Victoria you next." I was beaming as I showed my presents, an eight-inch doll made of plastic with movable arms and legs. Also a small carriage just fit for the doll. My mother had made the doll's dress and a tiny pillow and blanket for the carriage.

Vickie's doll was much larger with a porcelain head and a beautifully painted face. Mama had made a lovely corn blue muslin dress for her doll too. My sister Alma's gift was an exquisitely carved and painted music box. Ida received a diary with its own key, perfect for her, the secretive one in the family. Gottliebe's gift was a lovely hand-painted shawl and combs for her beautiful long black hair. Mama's gift from Papa was heavenly, a dress she didn't have to make herself and a black shawl with fringe on the bottom. Papa received a warm fur hat, the kind Russians still wear to this day in the winter. This was the first time our father could afford to buy all of us store-bought presents.

Later our sister Emma and her husband Gottlieb joined us for refreshments and the exchanging of the personal gifts. They lived with his parents in the same village, while Anna the oldest lived in Constanta, too far to come home for Christmas Eve. They would join us Christmas day for dinner.

Maria Reule Woelfl

"It's getting late," Mama said. "If you girls have gifts to exchange, you better get to it now, because it's past your bed time. One by one each girl went to her own special hiding place and brought out gifts she had made for our parents and each other. Gottliebe had knitted gloves for Mama and socks for Papa. Ida knitted them scarves in different colors. Alma made two handkerchiefs, a big one for Papa, and a smaller lovely embroidered one for Mama. Victoria drew two pictures; one was a vase with flowers for Mama, a horse and rider for Papa.

With Gottliebe's help I, Mariechen, wrote "I LOVE MAMA AND PAPA" on a piece of paper with colored pencil, and Gottliebe framed it. I was very proud presenting my gift to my parents. Mama made all of us new dresses from bolts of material Papa brought from the city. Mama gave Papa a sweater she knitted herself. Emma and her husband Gottlieb got small items for each of us. It was a wonderful and happy Christmas with everyone getting the perfect gift. We put all our presents under the tree and sang "Stiele Nacht, Heilige Nacht" once more. That night I dreamed of Kristkind and fairy princesses.

Christmas Day we all spent together. Anna, Johan and their daughter Maria came for Christmas dinner and so did Emma and Gottlieb. It was a lovely day. We had goose with all the trimmings and all kinds of pastries, and of course, happy chatter around the table. We sang Christmas carols afterwards, and you could feel the joy and abundant love flowing around and through us. We were all full from the big goose dinner and red cabbage, roasted potatoes and green beans and fruit compote. But we still enjoyed the dessert of Kuchen and Apple Strudel.

When it was time for Anna and Emma's families to leave, we wished each other "Frohe Weinachten," hugged and kissed through misty eyes, knowing this might be the last Christmas we would all spend together.

New Years day we all went "wishing." All the children went from house to house and wished all the German families Happy New Year. In return we each received a shiny new penny. Each child carried a little sack to put the coins in. The older boys and girls received a nickel or even a dime. Boys over eighteen were given a shot of Schnapps. After they made the rounds they had to go home to sleep it off. We walked everywhere so there was no chance of anyone getting hurt.

It was a great holiday season for all!

Maria, Gypsy Princess

Mama, Alma, Vickie, and Maria

Chapter 4

Now that the holidays were over, Mama was getting weaker every day. She sat in her rocking chair more often. I was always close, wanting to sit on her lap. She would send me outside to play. I was too young to realize how sick Mama really was.

I remember she was still with us in March when I celebrated my fifth birthday. She would get short of breath sometimes and had to sit and rest, but she wasn't bedridden or coughing too much yet. She still did most of her work up to the day she left.

Easter was also a big holiday for us but a sad one that year, because Mama was leaving soon. I didn't understand what that meant. Easter Sunday morning we had our breakfast then went to church to say prayers for Mama's health. Also, we went to rejoice that Jesus Christ ascended to a higher realm to be with his Father. After church we all went to the cemetery to put flowers on our loved ones' graves. Easter dinner was a ham or a pork roast with all the trimmings and always lots of sweet Easter baked goods too.

The week after Easter a car came and took Mama away. I wanted to go too, and I cried, holding onto her hand. Father held me back, telling me to let go. He said Mama was just going for a short ride and would be back soon. When evening arrived and it was time for bed, I cried more for Mama. In those weeks and months I missed Mama, asked for her constantly and wouldn't be comforted by my sisters, only Papa.

After Mama left for the hospital, father was our rock. Father knew how hard we all took it when Mama when away. At night after dinner he almost every evening would tell Vickie and me fairy tales at bedtime and Alma would come and listen too. I was a real night owl and never wanted to go to bed. Vickie was the opposite. She could hardly keep her eyes open when her head hit the pillow. She always snuggled deep into the featherbed and would be sound asleep in minutes.

Maria, Gypsy Princess

But Papa showed strain, and the laughter was gone from his eyes. We all walked around in a daze, wondering if Mama would come back. Life was more difficult now that she was gone. My sisters had their hands full with me. They came up with different stories every day why Mama wasn't with us. "Why?" I would say. "Why isn't Mama here? I want to go where she is." "Soon," they'd say, "we'll see her soon," but when soon didn't come and the next day she wasn't there, I got cranky and threw a tantrum. Papa was the only one who could quiet me.

I missed everything Mama did for me and with me. We all missed her cooking and her loving ways. She had always praised us for the littlest things we did. Even if she was disappointed in you, she found something nice to say. I missed her tucking me into my featherbed at night. The quilt she made from the soft plumage she plucked from our geese and ducks. She made my breakfast better then any of them could, and no one held me as lovingly as she had. They tried rocking me to sleep, but their laps were not the same. I would squirm around until they put me back down. All they tried was to no avail. I didn't want any part of it because it wasn't Mama's lap or her rocking or her singing voice. I usually wouldn't fall asleep until Papa came home and quieted me down. Vickie was also moping around as if she no longer belonged anywhere. She too was lost without Mama.

Life as we knew it was gone forever. Mama was the driving force behind us all. She was the sweetest person I ever knew.

****

It is strange how children in the same family can remember things so differently.

In 1988, we sisters met in Rumania for Anna's 70th birthday. It was quite an ordeal getting there. I flew to England first to meet up with Vickie. I stayed with her a few days then we took a flight to Constanta where Anna and her family lived. All five of us sisters were there.

The subject of mother's illness came up, and that's when I asked where our mother went when she left Rumania on that hospital ship. I was so young and the next years were so tangled by the war and so many changes, I never really knew where Mama went. My sisters told me she was taken to the town of Jadras in lower Austria near the Yugoslavian border. The area was called Steiermark and wasn't too far from Runn where we lived after we left the Cloister. Papa and Gotliebe visited Mama now and then for the next two years.

On another sisters' reunion, Vickie and I were talking about what a special person our father was, easy going and mellow. He never raised his hand to us or had a harsh word. Anna, Emma and Gottliebe remembered it differently. They

Maria Reule Woelfl

told us how strict Papa was with them when they were younger. If they didn't conform to his wishes, didn't do their chores or stayed out too late with their boyfriends, he got heavy handed and bellowed like a bull. There was always a switch nearby and sometimes he used it on them. Vickie and I knew he bellowed once in a while, but we thought his bark had no bite. They also told us Mama didn't have it so great. Papa was very demanding and jealous. When dinner wasn't ready on time he raised holly hell, and Mama got the brunt of it.

None of us knew how Father felt when our mother left. He didn't show his feelings to us. I know my entire family missed Mama. Especially Vicky, she and Mama had been very close too. My sisters told me later they didn't want to talk about Mama too much after she left so I wouldn't get to upset.

****

Turkish army Father on the left, unknown in the middle, Mothers brother on the right

Maria, Gypsy Princess

Our father had been in the Turkish army when he was younger. He was an interpreter because he spoke four or five different languages and dialects. Sometimes he told us stories about his army days. He learned to wrestle while he was in the Turkish army, and he was a good wrestler. There, it was for real, not like the shows they put on TV. He was really proud of his prowess in the ring. He also learned some Turkish songs he taught my older sisters, and they would put on a show on for us and sing Turkish songs and dance. They were good, and it was great fun to watch.

Father loved a party and after he had a couple of glasses of wine he would sing. They were old songs taught by the elders to the younger generation. Father was a self made man. He could do or fix anything he put his mind to. He made all my sisters' clogs. They were called Bantoffel in Bessarabia. He took a log and cut a thick slice and carved it into a sole. He then took a large piece of leather he had bought and cut it according to each girl's foot size. After that, he would put one their feet on the cut out piece of wood and draped the leather over it. Then he took really small nails and nailed the leather around their feet into the wood. That's all we would wear in the summer for work.

We had plenty of food, great meals, and our clothes were mostly hand-me-downs, more reasonable for a big family. Someone in the family bought big bolts of cloth in different prints, and the women made the same style dresses for all the cousins. The boys wore short pants until they were fourteen or so when they could wear long trousers. The short pants were mostly cut form older pants. In my age group, shoes were only worn in the winter, except Sundays or holidays. All the kids wore clogs or went barefoot in the summertime.

Baths were taken on Saturday in the summer kitchen when it was warm and then inside the kitchen in the winter. A big wash tub was filled with warm water and we bathed by age. When Mama was still with us, she would put me and Vickie in the tub first. Alma and Ida came next and so on, adding a little more hot water each time. After the girls were finished they hauled the water outside and poured it out. Then the tub was refilled with hot water so Mama and Papa could take their bath.

Father also made his own wine and Schnapps. The wine, of course, was made from grapes. Schnapps was made from all kinds of different fruit; apples, pears, plums and so forth. We picked up the fruit that fell on the ground and put it in a boiler Father had made out of a metal drum. Copper tubes ran down the side, and it was heated from the bottom with whatever he could find. The only drawback was a he had to use a lot of sugar, and sugar was dear.

Papa would have a shot of Schnapps every morning before he went out to feed the stock. "That's to get my heart started," he would say. He'd grin at us and go to work.

****

Cousin Rosa's wedding

A few months before we left Alakap, there was a double wedding in our family. A village wedding always caused a lot of commotion. Since most everyone was related it was a great big affair. All the women would prepare food for days, baking Kuchen, Strudel and all kinds of goodies. The wedding was held in the church then the whole party would walk through the village so everyone could see their finery and wish them good luck. It was very exciting and sometimes the celebration went on for days. The honeymoon was called the Bolder Wochen, weeks of honeymooning. Wedding talk reminds me of babies. In Rumania at that time babies didn't wear diapers as they do in this country. Instead a cloth was wrapped around the whole bottom half of the baby. The reasoning for that was the child would be bowlegged when it grew up if it wasn't done that way. Boy that must have been really uncomfortable having your legs tied down like that, plus being soaked all the way through. I know it happened to me but, of course, I don't remember.

Sometimes the mother would suckle the child until it went to school, and no one thought anything of it. There were a lot of superstitions in Bessarabia. Also a lot of home remedies for healing. For whooping cough, fever, boils, etc. remedies were made out of herbs, tree bark, berries and flowers. No doctors were close by, so home remedies cured a lot of sick people and were handed down from mothers to daughters, generation after generation. I still remember a recipe for curing boils.

You take a piece of yeast bread and chew it, then put it in a bowl and add a teaspoon of pork fat, a chopped clove of garlic, and slivers of lye soap. Mix the ingredients together and put it on the boil, then wrap your arm or leg with a piece of cloth and leave the poultice on for twenty-four hours. If the boil hasn't popped by then, repeat the whole process. The only problem was you had to walk around with a clothespin on your nose because it stinks to high heaven.

We might not have survived some illnesses if not for these remedies. For a cold or flu mix a cup of red wine with 4 cloves and 3 spoons of honey. Bring it to a boil, let it simmer a few minutes and drink it as hot as possible. Go to bed and perspire, and the next day you'll feel like a new person. The drink was also recommended for when you were snowed in. Sit close to a roaring fire and have a glass of "glow" wine.

When someone died the family wore black for a whole year and didn't dance or go to parties. The men wore a black band on their arms.

Our lives were simple, but about to become very complicated. The life we knew was soon too at an end, never to return. Hitler's war and his orders to leave our homes changed everything. Families were torn apart, separated for years. Some would never see each other again.

When the orders came, Anna, our oldest sister, her husband and daughter, Maria, still lived in Constanta by the Black Sea. Emma and Gottlieb lived with his parents, and she was pregnant with their first child, expecting any day. Emma and Gottlieb went to the same "Lager" as we did. Anna's family was taken to a different one near Poland.

Of course our mother was in an Austrian Hospital.

Chapter 5
Goodbye Alakap - October, 1940

The night before we were to leave for Austria, I dreamed I was sitting on my mother's lap in her rocking chair. I was crying. Mama rocked me, and was stroking my hair, "Hush, hush, my little one, don't be frightened. Mama is here to protect you." In the dream I snuggled closer to her and was content.

Suddenly the rocking became more violent. Instead of back and forth, I was moving sideways and the whole house shook. I woke and sat straight up in bed, confused as to where I was. Beside me, Vickie sat up, screaming,

"Hurry, Mariechen, it's an earthquake. We must get out!"

There was a loud crash as an oil lamp fell from the wall and shattered. Splinters of glass flew every which way. Good thing the lamp wasn't lit or there would've been a fire. From her bed in the corner Gottliebe shouted. "Mariechen, Vickie, be careful! Glass is everywhere. Don't step on it."

Doors banged open, and the others came out of their rooms.

"Halt! Don't move," father bellowed. "Gottliebe, get your clogs, put on your coat. Grab a blanket. Wrap Mariechen and carry her to the yard. The rest follow. Hurry, before the roof comes down!"

He ran back to his bedroom, grabbed some papers and a coat, and then joined us.

"Is everyone out?" he asked as he came through the door.

"Yes Papa, we're all here," we said in unison. The five of us stood there in our night clothes. Seventeen-year-old Gottliebe was in charge now, but we all missed Mama. How she would've calmed us.

It was late October and very cold. Father took me in his arms, and stood with my sisters in the middle of the yard, feet stuck in limestone muck, waiting for the earth to stop its tremors. The ground had been frozen the evening before, but it had rained during the night and now the yard was a gooey mess. We were all shivering, even Papa.

"Papa," I whimpered, "is our house going to fall down?"

"No, liebling, it will quit shaking soon, and we'll be able to go back inside." We stood in the cold mud for quite awhile before the aftershocks subsided. "Where is Mama, Papa? Why isn't she here with us?"

"We are going where mama is. Don't cry. We will see her soon."

Once back in the house, Papa took out a glass and poured himself a generous shot of Schnapps. "To get my heart started," he said and drank it down with one swallow. Besides the lamp that had shattered, there was no other damage. All our belongings were already packed into trunks, boxes and suitcases, and most of it already loaded on the wagon and covered with a tarpaulin. We were to leave early that morning in a horse drawn wagon.

Gottliebe lit the kitchen stove and made hot chocolate. Then she started breakfast and put a pot of water on the stove so we could wash, especially their muddy feet. We sat at the table, quiet a moment, then said a prayer, thanking God we were all safe and praying for our mother's health, and to be reunited with her soon.

"Thank you God for your blessings and grant us a safe trip," we prayed.

****

Our destination was the river Danube, the port of Cera-Voda, about fifty miles away. There we would board a ship for Smilline, Belgrade and from there a train to the town of Geras in Austria.

After we ate, we loaded the last of our belongings on the wagon and began our journey.

In the small village of Alakap were about thirty-seven families, 178 people of German decent, most were related by blood or marriage that had to leave there homes for good. Alakap had only been in existence for about forty years. The first settlers had a hard life forging existence out of barren land. They did it and reared their children and were sad to leave all they had accomplished behind. The land was barren and cold again. It was a sad sight to see, thirty-seven homes empty. No crops would be planted in the spring. They had sold most of the animals and land, but the dogs missed their owners and howled for attention. The families had to turn away.

We had no idea exactly where we would end up or how long we would be there. We were promised homesteads in the German occupied territories, but no one knew where or how long we would have to wait for a new home.

I don't remember much about the ship voyage. Either it was uneventful or there was so much going on my little mind couldn't absorb it all. When we docked in Belgrade we were put on a train to the town of Garas in Austria. I do remember that town and the Cloister. We were housed in an ancient monastery, a cloister. Whole families were now living in small, cold stone cubicles, which the monks had lived in. Most of the families stayed in the cloister for two years before the authorities found homesteads for them.

The monastery was solidly built with a big iron gate that, when closed and bolted, made the compound a fortress. In front, stood a small chapel with a tall steeple and stained glass windows and beside the chapel was a cemetery where the monks were buried. A small door in the gate opened so we could walk through into a huge courtyard. There was a stable for horses and other farm animals. In the back of the building was a huge garden with patches of fresh vegetables and fruit trees, a high stone wall around it. The garden and monastery had been self-sustaining and efficiently run by the monks. Now, the place would be run by the women of our families.

The garden reminded me of the Garden of Eden. An old gnarled apple tree stood the middle, its branches spread in all directions, laden with beautiful red apples. If I squinted just so, I could see the serpent wound around the trunk of the big old tree. He had fiery eyes and hissed through his fangs, telling Eve to give Adam the apple. When my imagination got the better of me, I'd run as fast as I could like a scared rabbit and slam the gate shut.

The Nazi regime had taken over the monastery a few years before, for the sole purpose of making it temporary housing for families like us. A large hall on the one side of the monastery was used for community dining and important meetings we were required to attend. The Nazi officers made sure we were all at the meetings. Once a week everyone met in the big hall to watch films of Adolf Hitler speaking to the nation. In the evening the adults, mostly men would sit in the same hall for hours listening to the radio propaganda of the SS.

There was an immense kitchen in the rear of the hall was where the women did the cooking for the whole group. Every morning, noon and evening we gathered in the dining hall and sat at long banquet style tables to eat our meals. The food was good because there were still fresh vegetables in the garden, potatoes, carrots, beans and pumpkins. We also enjoyed fresh fruit with our meals. Also pigs, chicken, geese and sheep were slaughtered for food.

The older men went out and found work wherever they could. Of course, the young strapping lads were drafted into the German army and sent to the front. The young women took jobs in local households or in the fields. All the children from age six to fourteen went to school right there in the monastery with thirty some pupils crowded into one classroom. The room must have been used as a classroom by the friars because it was set up for a schoolroom. The teacher had his hands full teaching so many different classes from first through sixth grade.

From time to time father took short trips and when I asked Gottliebe where Papa was, she told me he was visiting Mama.

"Why can't I go too," I asked.

"Mama is too ill, she said, "Papa will bring you kisses from Mama when he comes back, okay?" I still grumbled, but was happy I would get kisses from Mama.

Mama in the hospital she is the third person from the left

Life in the Cloister

Our new "home" was cold and dark, a twenty by thirty-foot stone. The furnishings consisted of one double bed and two smaller beds, a small dresser, small square table with two chairs and in the corner a potbelly stove. By the door was a wooden stand to hang our hats and coats on. This cramped room was to be our "Home sweet home" for now. This is where the five of us girls slept. Because our mother wasn't with us, Father slept with a group of bachelors on the other side of the monastery.

It was difficult to become accustomed to our new surroundings, especially for me being the youngest. I was frightened most of the time because the place was dreary and dark, and I was afraid to leave the room alone. Even Vickie and Alma, who were much older didn't care to walk through the dark corridors alone, because there were rumors that a ghost haunted it. We knew a monk was still residing in the cubicle next to ours. I never saw him, but at night a light would shine under the door and sometimes we heard shuffling sounds like someone having a hard time walking. We also heard papers rustling and a low murmuring, a Latin chant or prayer, coming from that room.

Vickie, Alma and I always held hands and ran as fast as we could through the corridor. The first night was the worst. There was a storm, the wind howling outside, and I was terrified. We were alone in the cold scary room. I begged Gottliebe to leave the light on. "Oh, Mariechen," she smiled, "don't be silly. There's nothing to be afraid of. We are all here. Just cuddle close to Vickie and go to sleep. Hold her tight and you'll be safe."

There was no bathroom close by so Gottliebe set a pail in the corner in case we had to use it during the night. I fell asleep wishing Mama were there to hold me. I dreamt I was on a boat, and water was splashing in getting Vickie and me all wet. I tossed in my sleep calling, "Mama, Mama, I'm drowning, help me."

Vickie woke and shook me. "Mariechen, you're all right. You're just dreaming. See you're right here in bed with me." Then she felt the sheet. "Oh, Maria, what did you do? I'm soaking wet and so are you. Oh, Lord! Now what? We don't have any dry sheets or nightgowns. They're still packed away."

"I'm sorry. I was scared. I dreamed I was drowning. I didn't realize I wet the bed." I was ashamed I hadn't wet the bed in years.

"Okay, don't cry. I'll wake Gottliebe. She'll think of something."

Gottliebe was rather disgruntled being awakened in the middle of the night, but she came up with a solution. She made us take off our nightgowns and slip into our undershirts. As we stood on the cold floor, shivering, Gottliebe turned the mattress over, put a couple of towels on it and reversed the covers so the wet part was on the outside. She told us to get back into bed.

The next morning I didn't want to leave the room. I thought surely, just by looking at me, everyone would know I had wet the bed.

"Mariechen, don't be foolish, Gottliebe said. "We won't tell anyone. Promise, okay?"

"I don't trust Vickie! She always tells her best friend Frieda everything."

"I won't tell a soul, cross my heart and hope to die," said Vickie.

They coaxed me awhile, and I finally agreed to go with them. Thinking of breakfast made me hustle. I was hungry!

The next morning there was a big uproar outside as a huge army truck thundered through the gate. Everyone ran outside to see what was happening. The truck stopped just inside the gate, and we were amazed at what we saw. Soldiers were busily throwing our luggage out on the ground, not caring whether they broke all our china or glassware. The few goods we could bring, so painstakingly packed away by the women, were now being thrown to the ground without care.

My father walked to the truck and shouted, "Achtung, Halt!" They stopped and saluted. They thought an officer was addressing them. "What are you doing? Are you crazy? Those are our belongings! You'll break every dish and glass in those cases. Please be more careful. If you can't do a decent job, get down from there and we'll do it ourselves."

Suddenly there was a lot of commotion as everyone headed toward the truck, wanting to climb on and look for their belongings.

"Hold it!" Father shouted, "Let's do this orderly." He called out four names. "Come on, you get on the truck and hand the luggage down to us. We can sort it all out after everything is off the truck."

They worked as a team and everything was off the truck in no time and nothing was broken. Then the luggage was sorted and taken to each family's room. The unloading and sorting was an all day job, but worth it. The women and girls went back to the dining room to clear the tables and wash the dishes for the next meal.

The younger girls took charge of the little ones. They had their hands full keeping them away from the workers. Everything was done in a group, and since most of us were related or friends, it all went smoothly.

Garas was a small town and the people who lived there didn't like us and treated us with cool disdain. Although we remained mostly in the abbey, the villagers told their children not to play with us. They called us names and sometimes even threw stones at us.

They thought because we came from Rumania we were wandering Gypsies. Gypsies had a bad reputation and people mistrusted them. There were a lot of Gypsies where we came from, and they stole anything they could lay their hands on, chickens, eggs, even pigs. The farmers were wary of them.

My sister, Emma, had gone into labor on way to the river Danube, and her son, Helmut, was born on top of the wagon en route to the ship. A midwife was with her, but it was a hard delivery. Just a few years ago Emma told me she almost died from loss of blood. She was very sick on board ship and after we arrived in Geras. She and Helmut were hospitalized, and she had to stay in bed almost a month. The baby was also sickly, but thank God they both survived and are still alive today. Anna, her husband Johannes and their daughter Maria where sent to a different "Lager" because they left Rumania from Constanta. We had no idea where they were at that time. Only later did we learn they ended up in Poland.

Maria Reule Woelfl

It is difficult to remember the details all of the other families. There were many ups and downs for everyone. Maybe it wasn't as difficult on our family because there weren't any boys. I know it was hard for the families whose sons were drafted into the German army. Many of my cousins were fighting in the war and some didn't come back.

I was a lonely, sensitive child and missed my mother's comforting arms around me. I cried often, particularly when boys teased me, which was almost every day. I thank God for my sisters who were all good to me. But they were so much older and had their own lives. They got tired of me constantly tagging along after them, so I spent a lot of time alone playing with my dolls.

I loved my father and he loved me, but he, too, was very busy man and didn't have much time to spend with me and since he slept on the other side of the cloister, most days we only saw him at meals. I really missed him. Every once in a while papa would come to our room in the evening and tell us some fairy tales. He would sit on our bed and Vickie and I would cuddle close to him and felt his warmed. Even Alma, at eleven, would sit and listen and Vickie almost always felt a sleep and Alma's head was also knotting. Those evenings I was very content and pretended I was the princess who lived happily-ever after and it felt great to be alive. When I spent time with my cousin Edmund, he and I were the same age and inseparable in Rumania. But as we got older, he didn't want to be seen holding my hand any more because other kids would tease him. They'd chant, "Edmund and Mariechen are in love," and Edmund would get red in the face and strike out at who ever was closest. I missed his friendship too.

I was lucky that all of my aunts were willing to take me in and treat me like one of their own. I remember my aunt, Paulina, would say, "It makes no difference if there eight or ten around the table, there's always enough to feed a couple more mouths." I was a child of the world, reared by my sisters and my aunts.

After the first big snow my sister, Vickie, had a close call with death. One day after school she was playing in the yard, throwing snow balls at the boys and chasing after them when she suddenly bent over and crumpled into the snow, holding her side and screaming. Everyone was terrified. We couldn't figure out what was wrong with her. One of my cousins ran and got his mother and luckily a German officer happened to be visiting at the time and came out too see what was going on. When he saw Vickie he scooped her in his arms, put her in the back seat of his car and told his driver to take them to the hospital. My Aunt Bertha and my sister Ida went with them. As the car drove off, Ida hollered out the window, "Mariechen, go find Papa and have him come to the hospital."

The hospital was twenty miles away and they arrived just in time to save Vickie's life. Her appendix had ruptured, and when they cut her open it was already spread through her system. If Officer Schultz hadn't been there, she would have died. He saved Vickie's life. Vickie remained in the hospital an extra week because a severe snowstorm closed the roads. When she came back she had some interesting stories to tell us. She had helped the sisters take care of sick and wounded soldiers. She came home happy and smiling. She had also gained weight because they fed her ice cream at every meal. She enjoyed being pampered and thought it a great adventure. After that we called her Roll-Mopes because she had such full rounded cheeks.

After a year living in the cloister, my father became impatient with the bureaucrats who kept putting him off saying, "soon" every time he asked when we would be placed in a permanent home. When he couldn't stand the living conditions or the run-around any longer, he took off on his own and found us a homestead in Yugoslavia near the Austrian border. The property he acquired had a big white house with ivy growing up its walls and green shutters on the windows. The ivy was so thick you could hardly see the white paint on the house. A lot of land went with the house, for planting and growing vegetables, not only for our own consumption but for marketing. Gardening was my father's occupation. He grew vegetables and a variety of flowers, there was a hothouse in the garden to cultivate exotic flowers to sell. Because of the war it was a lucrative business. A year after leaving Rumania, we moved to Runn by the River Save in Yugoslavia. We left our sister, Emma, and her son and all our other relatives behind. No one knew where they might end up. Within two years the authorities found homes for all the families.

They were scattered all throughout Europe.

Chapter 6
1941, The Train for Yugoslavia

It was mid October when our father returned from his trip to Yugoslavia.

He was really excited because he found the most wonderful place for us to homestead. He told us (and anyone standing near) how beautiful the town and our house and land were, and how big everything was.

We repacked the belongings we had with us at the cloister. The bulk of our stuff was never unpacked. Everything was loaded on a wagon and father and me by his side, drove us to the train station. We had said our good byes at dinner the night before, a quiet celebration and bittersweet because we were leaving our family. The whole village hadn't been separated from each other since birth. Our lives from now on would be different, and many tears fell that day. Our sister, Emma, and the other four girls went in a different wagon, and Emma bid us God speed at the station.

Emma went back to Garas to wait to be placed into a homestead with her baby son, Helmut. Her husband was in the German army, and no one knew where he was or when he would return. She was alone to carry on. It was a sad farewell. We didn't know when or if we would ever see them again.

As it turned out they were placed into a homestead in Czechoslovakia a year later. Our oldest sister, Anna, and her daughter, Maria, ended up in Poland while Johan was at war. Ida and I were the only ones who saw Emma two years later and a year after that we were reunited with Anna. Most of the family didn't see their relatives again for over forty years. Anna and her family stayed behind in Rumania and could not come out until the 1980's. Our father never saw Anna, Emma or their families again.

Yugoslavia!

We all loved the house in Runn. Everything about the place was great. It was big and roomy with lots and lots of land, more than we expected, and we could not believe our luck. Life would to be good for us now. We knew we would miss our big family, but it was a great and new adventure, and I, for one, loved it.

By the time we all settled in, it was in late October before Vickie, Alma and I went to school. I had a late start, and it was difficult to catch up with the rest of the class. It was very different from the school we attended in Garas. I started first grade and Vickie, fifth or sixth and Alma went to high school. Gottliebe took over the household and took care of us as she had when we lived in Rumania after our mother left. With Ida's help, they did the cooking, washing and all the other chores. They had to work in the fields and in the florist business too. I think Gottliebe and father went to visit Mama in the hospital a few times. They didn't talk about her much. They probably didn't want to upset me.

Across from our house was a barn for the horse, cow and chickens. We had fresh eggs, milk and sometimes even a chicken dinner. We also raised rabbits for food, and they were very tasty. Runn was all father had said and more. The house had a big kitchen, a large round table in the middle and six chairs around it. A stove was in one corner, a china cabinet in the other, and a big wash basin with running water, the running water is something we didn't have when we lived in Rumania. The living room and two bedrooms faced the front of the house, the living room in the center The "outhouse" was inside off the hallway by the front door. On the other side of the bathroom, a staircase led to an attic bedroom. We all really appreciated that in winter when we no longer had to go outside and freeze our butts off to go to the bathroom. Alma slept in the attic room while Vickie and I shared a room downstairs, and Papa slept in the other bedroom. Next to the stable across the street was a small apartment where Gottliebe and Ida slept.

Life went smoothly. Father hired workers to tend the garden and flower beds, a variety of seedlings growing under glass covers. Also they worked the fields, planting and harvesting vegetables.

School was more difficult than kindergarten, and I didn't to do well. The kids made fun of me because I had a different German dialect. They teased and I was always crying. Although my teacher was nice and I liked her, I still had a hard time of it. It took about a year before I finally made some friends. Things got easier then, and I started to love school.

We had a rabbit pen behind the house, and I loved to go and play and talk to them. The pure white one was a mama rabbit and she was my favorite. I loved her, and she was going to have babies soon. Every day after school I went outside and took Emilie a carrot and told her I missed my mama, and I knew she would be happier after she had her baby rabbits. The first year in Runn I was a very lonely child. My sisters were always on the go, so until

Maria Reule Woelfl

I made some friends I spent a lot of time by myself. Also I wasn't taught hygiene and didn't know how to brush my teeth. I just put some salt on my finger and rubbed it across my teeth and gums to clean them. I remember my teacher asked us if we brushed our teeth every day, and I was ashamed to admit I didn't even have a brush. I never saw my sister Gottliebe brush, so I thought I didn't need to either. It was a very confusing time for me, and I felt I didn't belong anywhere.

At least one thing stayed the same. In the evenings after dinner, father would tell Vickie and me fairy tales. I loved listening to his voice. Being close to father was familiar and made me feel good. It was getting colder now so, to keep warm, I'd sit on top of the stove after the fire had burned out. Papa sat on a chair in front of me with Vickie next to him. He began, "Okay what do you want to hear tonight?"

"Rumpelstiskin," I would say.

"No, we heard that one last night," Vickie would say. "I want Snow White."

And I would say, "No, Hansel and Gretel." And so it went every evening. Being the youngest gave me the edge, and I got my way most of the time. Sometimes I would comb Papa's hair, Vickie sitting next to him.

Years later at one of our reunions, Vickie told me how she enjoyed it when father wrapped her long black hair around his finger and would twine it up then unwind it again. It made her feel loved and special, and it felt so good she almost always fell asleep. We talked about our mother too. She told me how close she had been to Mama, how she cried herself to asleep almost every night after mama left for the hospital. She still missed her every day.

Time seemed slower as we settled into our new routine. Then it was suddenly December and a lot of snow had fallen in the night. I, for one, loved it because we had fun throwing snow balls and sliding down hill on a sled. I didn't have a sled, but by then I had befriended a girl named Hildegard who lived across the street and had a shed. She and I would sled down the hill in front of our house. What fun we had. She admitted she was glad to have someone to help pull the sled back up.

I could hardly wait for Christmas, because I had asked Saint Nick to bring me a sled and ski pants and boots to go with it. When Christmas Eve Day finally came I was really excited, but it still seemed a long wait for Christmas Eve. Just as in the past, it was our time to celebrate. Vickie, Alma and I were kept in the kitchen, while father, Gottliebe and Ida decorated the tree in the living room and hid the presents.

When they came back, I tried to run to see what Saint Nick brought, but as usual I was held back because we had to eat dinner first. It wasn't quite the same without Mama. She always made everything special, and we all missed her. At dinner we added a special prayer for Mama, how we wished she were with us. Sitting and eating dinner was one of the longest hours I ever spent. When we finally finished, no one could hold me back! I ran into the other room, searching for that something special, but I couldn't find it.

There were wrapped packages under the tree, but I was looking for something bigger. I looked everywhere but to no avail. The candle lit tree was on top of the dining room table, and a white tablecloth hung to the floor. My sisters tried to give me a hint. They looked at me, then the floor, nodding toward the table, but I just couldn't make the connection. Finally Gottliebe couldn't stand it. She took my hand, pulled the table cloth up, and there was the most beautiful sled I had every seen.

I pulled it out and headed for the door, but my father grabbed me by the back of the collar. "Oh, no Where do you think you are going? It's dark outside. You can't go sledding until the morning."

I was always the last out of bed, but not that morning. I couldn't wait to get dressed and have breakfast. Then I was out of the house like a shot! Now that I had the sled, I made more friends because they all wanted to ride it. I felt very important, beaming and grinning from ear to ear.

Christmas was over so preparation for New Years began. It wasn't like in Rumania or even Geras Austria. We had a quiet evening with a special dinner, and later the older girls went out with their boyfriends. Alma, Vickie and I stayed home and after father told us some fairy tales, he too went out to bring in the New Year with friends. The three of us stayed home and listened to the radio.

I enjoyed my sled after school. I rode it down the street in front of our house. Going down the hill took me a few minutes, but coming back was another story, a lot of huffing and puffing pulling it back up. I didn't care. I stayed out all afternoon sledding until they had to call me in for supper. The next months went by fast, and on March 8th my sister threw me a birthday party. I was seven. Birthdays were very special in our family, and my sisters invited a few friends from school and some neighborhood kids to the party.

Our mother was still sick in the hospital, and that made me sad, but we all prospered. The city of Runn was in the occupied German territories of Yugoslavia, which was invaded by them earlier in the war. It wasn't far from where Tito's partisans were fighting the German army in the hills. The battles were severe with many German casualties. The partisans would strike, and then disappear as if swallowed up by the earth. Since the partisans knew everyone in the area, the people hid them. So it became hide-and-seek, strike-and-run situation. The good thing about living where we did, there weren't as many airplanes flying over. But there was always the threat of bombs falling.

I fell behind in first grade because my sisters didn't give me enough attention with my homework. When I brought my first report card home I was excited to show my father. He looked at it then passed it on. It went all around the table without anyone saying a word. I watched and waited, expecting someone to say, good job Mariechen, but instead they started to laugh.

Gottliebe said, "I wouldn't be so proud, Mariechen. You didn't even pass the first grade."

I looked left and right then at my father. "Papa, is that true?" He just nodded, held out his arms to me, and I went to him and started to cry. It was as if my heart was breaking. I buried my face against my father's shoulder and cried until my whole body shook. My sisters came and said they were sorry and they would help me from now on. They put the job on Vickie because she was the best student. She grumbled saying she already had too much work of her own, and couldn't take on more. Alma said she would take up the slack. They were talking about me as if I wasn't even in the room. I asked my Father to take me to bed. That made my sisters takes notice because it was the first time I ever asked to go to bed without being told or be coaxed. Papa carried me to my bedroom, lay me on the bed and kissed my cheek.

He said, "I'll send Gottliebe to help you get undressed and put you to bed. Don't cry anymore. It will be all right in the morning. I love you, sleep well."

The next day all my sisters were very sorry they had laughed at me. They promised never to do it again, and I forgave them.

Alma had turned sixteen March 26th, and wanted to go out with a young man she had met at a tailor shop where Papa had his clothes made. Father said she was too young for a boyfriend. So she came up with the idea of asking Ida to go out with Mathias' friend, Joseph. They were both apprentices in the same tailor's shop.

Alma figured since Ida was two years older and could have a boyfriend, they could go out as a foursome. Father would surely let the four of them go to a movie. It worked, and the following Saturday evening they went to a movie. Father lay down the law; the latest they could stay out was 10:00 o'clock. Alma didn't care as long as she could be with Mathias.

From then on, summer was a lot more fun because Ida, Alma, Mathias and Joseph became inseparable, and they took Vickie and me with them on picnics. There was a great beach by the river Sava where we went swimming. The river flows through a lot of countries, starting in Austria, then Yugoslavia then on to Switzerland.

That summer I almost drowned. While the others swam in the river, I was playing in the shallow water picking up stones to take home. I kept going a little farther into the water to find shiny stones, when suddenly I stepped wrong and the current took me in its grasp, moving me to the middle of the river and pulling me under. When I bobbed back up I sputtered and screamed in panic. Joseph heard and saw I was in trouble. He raced in and swam downstream. He got to me just before I went under the third time. I

Maria, Gypsy Princess

had swallowed a lot of water, but Joseph pulled me up by my hair and carried me ashore. He lay me down, and Ida gave me mouth to mouth and revived me. Water came spurting out, and I felt awful. Thank God for Joseph. If not for his quick thinking, that might've been the end of my life. I've been scared of deep water ever since.

It was a good summer and life went along at a steady pace. Fall approached and soon it was back to school.

Father took a short trip to visit Mama in the hospital, and he was told Mama would be sent home soon. When I found out my excitement was at fever pitch. Time was going too slow waiting for her arrival. Of course, I had no idea Mama was still very sick. When we saw her we were shocked how she had changed the last three years. She looked haggard, her hair peppery and dull, but her smile was the same. I wanted to hug her, but I was held back and told that Mama was too sick to be hugged. I started to cry. Mama said, "Libeling don't cry. I love you. Come here; let me hold your hand." That brought my smile back.

We were surprised they let her come home. Her tuberculosis was very contagious and she was still very ill. Her disease had worsened over the years.

So why was she coming home? Did Mama come home to die? We found out she was dying and had come home to say farewell to her family. Allowing that was the most irresponsible thing the doctors could do. A nurse should have come with her to care for her.

After they settled Mama in the attic room, Vickie and I went up to see her. She was coughing and could hardly talk. She told us not to come to close. "But Mama, we haven't seen you for so long." When we tried to move closer, she kept saying, "Nein, nein ich bin zu krank, Bitte bleibed weider weck von mir." No, no, stay away. I am very sick. Don't come too close."

My sister, Ida, had to take care of mama. Mama was spitting up green and yellow mucous and blood. She was spreading the infectious decease. Ida was exposed to it every day and caught the worst of it. Vickie and I also spent a lot of time upstairs with Mama, and we were infected too. Mama was coughing all the time and in pain. The sisters kept telling me to stay out of Mama's room, but I wouldn't listen. As soon as they went to work and Ida stepped out for fresh air, I snuck up to be near Mama. Of course she kept telling me not to come close and sent me out, saying she was tired and had to rest.

After awhile our regular doctor came to see her and couldn't believe they would send such a sick woman home to infect her children. We asked Papa why Mama was sent home. He said she wanted to see her children one more time and say goodbye.

Still she should have been in a hospital close by so we could see her there. The damage was done, and it was too late to change the outcome now. Father found out the Gestapo told Mama's doctors since she wasn't getting better they might as well send her home too say goodbye to her family.

Our regular doctor felt sorry for us and prescribed a new medication for Mama. But when Gottliebe went to have it filled, the druggist said he could not fill it because it was laced with poison.

I overheard my father and Gottliebe talking, and Papa said, "Oh I don't think it is poisonous, you must have heard him wrong."

She said, "I don't know but he wouldn't give it to me."

"Well," Papa said, "why don't you go back to the doctor and see what he has to say about it." While Gottliebe was gone, I went upstairs and told Mama what I overheard and pleaded with her not to take the medication.

("ON MEIN LIEBLING ICH BIEN SO KRANK ICH WILL NICHT MAR LEBEN. ICH MOCHTE LIEBER INSCHLAFEN UND NICHT MAR AUFWEGEN!" "My love, I am so ill, I don't want to live any longer. I just want to go to sleep and never wake up again."

I told Vickie and she said, "Oh, Mariechen, you must have heard wrong. I am sure that isn't so."

Well, she didn't believe me, so I went to Gottliebe and begged her not to let the doctor give Mama the medicine, but it was to no avail. The doctor came the next day and gave Mama a spoon full of the stuff, and she was dead in a few hours. To this day no one will admit they gave her that medication.

It was a very sad time for all of us. We had lived almost three years without our mother, and then to send her home just to die was a hard blow, especially for me. I was finally making some friends and feeling better about myself. Now I felt awful because I was losing Mama all over again and this time for good.

Was this hurt ever going to go away? I wasn't sure, and the emotional roller coaster was starting all over again. I was crying a lot and calling for Mama in my sleep. I knew this time she wouldn't come back to us, and I didn't want to be comforted. I wanted my Mama. It was a quiet funeral with family and a few of father's friends and workers. I can still see the cemetery in my mind, the deep black hole Mama was put into. It hounded me, and at night I dreamed of it.

This poem struck me as so true.

Ever has it been
That love knows
Not its own
Until the hour of separation
Kahlil Gibran

This poem is from a book of "Meditations,"

Maria, Gypsy Princess

Published in Australia, this edition was published 1994 for Selecta Book Ltd,

My sister Vickie gave me the book on my birthday a few years before she died.

It was a long sad fall, September now and school was starting within weeks. I wasn't looking forward to it and went back a lonely child again. Sometimes after school, I would sneak up to the attic room and lay on the bed where Ida slept while she took care of Mama. I lay there thinking of the past when I was four and sat on mama's lap, rocking in the rocking chair she loved so much, and I stared at Mama's empty bed, and cried myself to sleep. My sisters knew they could find me there when they came home from the fields.

Life is so precious. We have to hold onto every moment with all our might and not let go too easily. The memory lingers on and my mother is always in my heart. Our life went on, but it wasn't the same without Mama.

Ida and Joseph got engaged in December, 1942 and were married in February, 1943. I think she was pregnant and Father made Joseph marry his daughter. The wedding was a small, quiet affair. They took a short trip to Austria for their honeymoon. Joseph had been drafted so he had to come right back and leave for the army. Later we found out he went into the S.S.

Ida caught the disease from Mama and was sick now, and as soon as Joseph left for the front, she went into the same hospital where our mother had been.

Ida & Joseph's wedding, Maria and Lorie, Mathias as best man

Chapter 7

In February, 1943, right after Ida's wedding, Father took a vacation. It was a trip to Germany to visit an old friend Hans Stollmaker also from Rumania that lived in the city of Dresden now. While he was in Germany, he met a lady named Elise Beier Nee Stroblet. She was visiting her brother and my father's friend, Hans was also from Alakap, and they had gone to school with my father. Hans and his wife, Erika, moved to Germany in the late 1935.

Hans gave a party for his friend, Gottliebe, and invited some of his new friends to meet him. Among them was Elise's brother, Kurt, who had brought Elise to the party. Father was smitten with her right away and while there, he and Elise were able to spend a few chaperoned days together and get to know each other better.

Elise was a widow with three children, a boy named Eberhard, Kurt Joachim Beier was eleven, and two daughters, Renate, fifteen and Helga, thirteen. I wasn't keen on the idea of Father bringing all these new people into our lives, but what could I do? I was only a child no one listened to. I always loved my birthday but my eighth birthday was a sad one. Mama gone, and Papa bringing a new family into the house made it impossible to be happy.

A month or so later Father sent Gottliebe to bring the whole Beier family to Runn. It was quite a shock to me when they actually arrived, and I was very angry and hurt that Father would bring another woman into our home, with three children, yet!

How could he be so mean? Didn't he know how much I loved him and that I didn't want to share him with anyone else? She is going to ruin everything, I thought, and take him away from me, from us. So I cried myself to sleep that night and a few nights after.

There was a lot of excitement over the next few weeks. The household was turned upside down with rearranging furniture and figuring out where everyone was going to sleep. The house just wasn't big enough for all of us.

The stove was moved into the front room and the kitchen was made into a bedroom.

Now that Ida was gone, Alma moved in with Gottliebe. Elise, Helga, and Renate slept in the kitchen area. It was big enough for two double beds. Vickie and I stayed in the same room for now and Eberhard slept upstairs. It was quite a change for all of us, but we had to make do.

We had to call Elise "Mutti" now, and from then on we called our Father "Vati." Calling Papa Vati was Mutti's idea. It sounded better to her and the names matched. As I said, there were a lot of changes, and I, for one, didn't like any of them. The food Mutti cooked was different than what we were used to, and even Vati started complaining after a week. Gottliebe had to teach Mutti how to cook our way.

I liked Eberhard but had nothing in common with the girls or Mutti. She had too many rules. Now I had to go to bed at 7:00 in the evening. That was way too early for me. Also Vati spent his evenings with her now, and our story telling was a thing of the past. I was never alone with Vati anymore, and that caused me a lot of pain. Everything was changing too fast. We didn't even have enough time to grieve for Mama, and Ida was gone now too, and I missed her. All we had left was a house full of strangers.

Easter was late that year, the first week in April, and I was looking forward to it.

The Rabbit and the Silk Dress

Easter morning I awoke to the aroma of fresh baked caramel-raisin-nut rolls. It made my mouth water.

I was eight years old now, with short blond hair and big velvet brown eyes.

When I awoke, I jumped out of bed and raced to the corner where the night before I had made a nest of real grass. I was all excited to see what the Easter Bunny had brought me. In the nest were colored eggs, chocolate covered candy and all kinds of little goodies.

I didn't believe the Bunny laid the colored eggs because we raised rabbits and I knew they didn't lay eggs. But I still got excited and enjoyed all the goodies on Easter.

I got dressed and went into the kitchen where I found Gottliebe setting the table for breakfast.

"Sit down, Mariechen," she said, "as soon as everyone is here, we'll eat."

I sat at the big round table, anxious to bite into a delicious sweet smelling roll.

Mutti, our stepmother, came through the door carrying a sky blue silk dress.

"Mariechen," she said, "this dress used to belong to Renate and then to Helga when they were your age and it is still like new. I want you to wear it to church today, okay!"

"Thank you," I said. It was a pretty dress but not my style. She hung the dress on the door and sat down. Victoria said grace and we ate breakfast. There was happy chatter around the table. Vickie was asking me what the Easter bunny brought me and I told her about the rainbow colored eggs. After we finished we all left for church.

As soon as the Easter service was over and we said our good-byes to the minister and some friends, Vati hustled us to our carriage. Vati and Kurt sat in the driver's seat while the seven of us crowded into the back seats, me on Gottliebe's lap. Vati cracked his whip, and said, "Giddy-up, Heidi, let's go home!"

The streets were quiet except for the clip clop, clip clop the horse's hooves made on the cobblestones. I closed my eyes and let the rocking of the carriage lull me into reverie. I was thinking of Emily, my white fuzzy rabbit who was just about to have babies, and I was anxious to get home to feed her... I was brought back from my musing by Mutti. "Mariechen," she said, be sure you take off that dress before you go chasing after your foul rabbits!"

Foul rabbits she says, what does she know about rabbits? She always picks on me not a moment's peace. This darn dress, I wish I had never laid eyes on it. I grant you, the dress was beautiful with embroidered lace around the collar and puffed short sleeves, but I was a tomboy and more comfortable in leader-hosen and climbing trees than a fancy dress.

As soon as the wagon stopped, Kurt jumped off and made a beeline towards the rabbit cage. He called to me, "Mariechen, hurry, your rabbit is loose!"

I jumped off Gottliebe's lap and raced across the yard to catch up with him, while Mutti shouted after me, "Maria, come back here and take off your dress first. "Get back here, your dress!"

Not slowing my pace, I chased after Emily. Kurt and I shooed her to the corner of the fence, and I grabbed her by the ears, scooped her up and carried her back to the cage. When I tried to pull her away from me, her claws held on tight. Kurt didn't notice that she was hanging onto me and grabbed her by the back of the neck and pulled her loose. When Kurt turned to face me again he pointed, "Oh my God, Mariechen, look at your dress!" Looking down, I gulped for air when I saw the damage Emily's claws had made. The dress was ruined! I felt sick to my stomach, and hot tears sprang to my eyes.

Maria, Gypsy Princess

"You're really going to get it," said Kurt," if I were you I'd run away right now."

"Oh, no, I can't do that," I said. "I always own up to what I do. It wasn't my fault, and I know if I tell the truth nothing bad will happen to me!"

"You don't think so? Just wait until my mother sees your dress," said Kurt and took off.

As I stepped through the front door, my sister Alma spotted me. "Oh my Lord, what happened to you?" she asked, and I repeated my story about chasing Emily. "Come on; let's change your dress before Mutti sees."

She took my hand – too late.

The kitchen door opened, and Mutti walked out, "Dinner is... Oh my God!" she yelled, pointing, "You ruined my beautiful dress!" She closed her eyes for a few moments and stood still, not uttering a sound. Alma and I didn't know what to do next.

I finally stammered, "I... I am, sorry, it wasn't..."

Suddenly Mutti's green eyes flew open, and the fire and anger I saw made me flinch. Her hand flew up to strike me. I covered my face with my hands waiting for the sting. It didn't come because Alma deflected the blow with her hand. With disdain, Mutti turned and stalked away.

Father heard the commotion from the kitchen. He opened the door and shouted, "What is going on out here? You're making enough noise to wake the dead.... Oh," he said and stopped when he saw my dress. "Mariechen, what have you done to your beautiful dress?"

I just stood there with quivering lips and tears rolling down my cheeks.

Vati said, "Now, now, Mariechen, stop crying. It isn't the end of the world. It's only a dress."

Then he scooped me up in his arms and wiped my tears with his handkerchief.

"Hush now, and don't worry. I'll talk to Mutti. Everything will be alright." Setting me back down, he said, "Alma, take her to her room. Help her change her clothes, and hurry because I'm hungry."

At dinner the atmosphere was cool and silent. Vati looked at me and said, "Mariechen, apologize to Mutti for ruining the dress."

"I am sorry, Mutti."

"Now," Vati said to Mutti, "Elise, you are the adult here, so no more nonsense about the dress, you hear?" He then bowed his head to say grace.

"Father, thank you for this bountiful food we are about to receive. Bless us, for we are thankful to be together on this Easter Sunday. Unite our families and remove all discord from this room and bind us into a strong union of love. Bring peace to our nation. Thank you, God!" We said Amen in unison. Vati looked around the table and picked up his fork and started eating.

Chapter 8

As time went by it got easier to follow the rules and Mutti did ease up a bit. It wasn't easy to please Mutti. Being brought up in a strict German family, her obsession was cleanliness, to the point of white glove treatment on the furnishings. None of us were clean enough for her.

I was becoming a regular tomboy. I saw a movie with a little girl in it, and they called her Peter and she wore Lederhosen. From then on I wanted to be called Peter too. My sisters laughed at me, but they did call me Peter for awhile, and it was fun to pretend.

So life went on. I had a friend, Gretel, and my brother, Eberhard, liked Gretel too, so we did a lot of things together. Her parents had a store so one day she brought a pack of cigarettes for the three of us, and we went to our barn and lit up. I took one drag and started to cough. It was the most awful tasting stuff, and I declared right then and there I would never smoke. I never did. I tried it again when I was seventeen and still didn't like it so that was the end of smoking.

Gretel didn't like smoking either, but Eberhard smoked the whole cigarette. We then played hide and seek, and I was to count to a hundred while they hid. After I finished counting I looked everywhere for them and called to them, but they didn't answer. I thought of looking in the hayloft, but there was no ladder. I couldn't climb up to look for them there.

So I went to our house, thinking they went there and left me behind but they were nowhere to be found. I went back to the barn and heard them giggling. They were up in the hayloft, after all. They climbed up the ladder then pulled it up behind them. I called up to them and asked what they were doing in the hayloft, and they said I was too young to understand.

I said, "I do know what you're doing. You're kissing and making out, that's what!"

They giggled louder, and Eberhard put the ladder back down. They called down to me that I could come up now. I was too mad at them so I went home talking too myself.

A few days later after our noon meal, my father asked Eberhard and me if we wanted to watch the florist garden that afternoon. He told us if we sold something we could keep the money. We were really excited about the prospect of making some money.

It was a slow day, and we got sort of bored with the whole thing when I spotted a man coming through the gate. I quickly went up to him and asked if I could help him.

He was taken aback because he said, "I would like to be taken to someone in charge. I am looking for a hothouse plant. I don't know what it's called, but I know what it looks like."

"Oh, can I help you? I am Maria. You know my father, don't you?"

"Oh yes, I know Herr Reule very well. You are his daughter?"

"Yes, I'm Maria Reule. My father put me and Eberhard in charge for the afternoon, and I can sell you whatever you need."

"Okay, he said, let's go inside and see if we can find what I am looking for."

In the meantime Eberhard came over to say hello and he wanted to help him.

I spoke up, "I'm already taking care of Herr… Herr…"

"Friedrich," he said.

"Yes," I said to Eberhard, "Herr Friedrich and I will get along just fine without your help, so don't bother us." We walked into the steaming hot room and started looking around. He indeed found the plant he wanted and picked it up. "How much?" he asked.

I looked on the bottom of the pot and found the price.

"That will be three DM, please, Herr Friedrich." He handed me five Deutche Marks, and I gave him change from the change drawer and put the five DM into my pocket and said,

"Goodbye. Herr Friedrich. Please come again."

After he was gone, I gave Eberhard the raspberry. "I have some money and you have none," I said, and pulled out the five DM, put it under his nose.

Eberhard tried to take it from me saying, "You didn't make five, Mark you only made 3.00, so put 2.00 back. Give it to me, he shouted." He tried to take it again, but I pulled back.

"I did too make 5.00 Mark," I said, "see, I have it right here in my hand."

"Put the money back." He shouted again.

Maria Reule Woelfl

I put the 5.00 Mark into my pocket and ran away. He kept shouting, "I'll tell," but I just kept going. I went to play with my friend, Heidi, until it was time to go home.

That evening Eberhard could hardly wait to tell everyone what I did. He told his mother first, and she agreed that I should give two Mark back. But I wouldn't hear of it.

"Just watch and see," I said, "I know when Vati gets home, and he'll let me keep it. Eberhard was still auguring and getting red in the face. He kept saying, "Make her give it back."

My Father said, "Stop shouting. What are you talking about? Give what back?"

"I told you, she should only keep three Mark, instead of all five."

"Oh that," Vati said, "She can keep all of it. After all she sold something so she has the right to keep it all." That made him even angrier and he started to sputter, but my father held up his hand and shouted, "Pasta, no more. Let's eat."

Eberhard didn't give up so easily and was still talking about it the next day. So to make peace I shared the money with him, and that made him happy.

****

There were air raids almost every day then, and our family lived in constant fear of bombs. When I was eight the most frightening experience in our lives occurred. Two of Tito's planes snuck in under the radar and raised hell. It happened on a bright sunny Sunday morning when our family of nine was sitting around the table having breakfast. We heard a plane approach. We felt the vibration as it roared over the house, making the windows rattle, and we all jumped up and raced to the window. The plane had zoomed out of sight by then, but we could still hear it.

I was standing next to my father. I pulled on his pant leg. "Vati, I can't see." He picked me up so I could look out. A second plane suddenly appeared out of the morning sun and headed straight for our house.

Father shouted, "Get down! Hit the floor!"

That's when we heard the rat-tat, rat-rat of rapid fire from a machine-gun. Papa dropped to the floor with me in his arms. At the same time, he pulled Vickie, standing next to him, down with us. My stepmother panicked. She shrieked, bolting forwards, but father grabbed her ankle and tripped her. As she fell she hit her head on a chair and lay face down in front of us. All the others were crouched under the second window or lying flat on the floor.

Maria, Gypsy Princess

Bullets shattered the windows, and glass splinters showered us like hail in a storm. Bullets whistled over our heads, embedding into the opposite wall. Finished with its job, the plane headed back to the hills where it came from.

The bombardment happened so fast, if it hadn't been for our father's split-second reaction, some of us might have perished in that foray.

"Is everyone all right?" father shouted.

"Yes," came all the reply from all directions.

"Stay on the floor," he ordered, "I'll go outside to see if the planes are gone." Quite a lot of time elapsed before he came back, and just as he came into the room the siren wailed the all clear.

He carefully walked around the glass and told us not to move so we wouldn't get cut. He took a broom and swept an area clean next to were my stepmother was lying. Afterward, he removed some glass from her hair and body then handed the broom to my sister, Gottliebe. "Here, see to the others," he said and went back to tend to Mutti. He turned her over and examined her injuries. Her temple was oozing blood and there were bruises around her wound. My father took a glass of water from the table and gave her a sip. He then dipped a napkin into the glass and tapped her wound asking if she was all right. She only nodded then painfully closed her eyes.

In the meantime, Gottliebe lifted me up and asked if I was okay. A small "Yes" came out of me. Gottliebe then swept a clear path on the floor for all of us to walk through. The memory of that day stayed with me. Vati told us the planes were Tito's. Tito was leading his guerrilla partisans against the Nazis and doing a lot of damage. The partisans knew the countryside well, and they would make fierce attacks then retreat into the mountains and the Germans couldn't find them. Eventually those partisans drove the German army out of Yugoslavia.

As time went on I buried the horrendous experience deep into my subconscious.

Until 1994 when I flew to Austria for my sister, Alma's fiftieth wedding anniversary. Four of us sisters sat reminiscing about our early lives and the subject of Yugoslavia came up. Then I recalled and mentioned that Sunday morning in 1943 when Tito's planes shot through our windows. We all sat quietly for a few moments, each in our own thoughts. In a few moments I said a prayer, thanking God for saving our lives and how grateful we were for this time we could spend together, also times yet to come.

Maria Reule Woelfl

Yugoslavia, the fall of 1943

Life went on and there were still a lot of disagreements between the two families. That year Eberhard, Helga and Vickie were drafted into the Hitler youth. I was too young, and that made me unhappy. They always told me how much fun they had going different places and learning all kinds of things. My sister, Vickie, was a very good student and wanted to become a teacher. When she turned sixteen in another year she would go to a special teaching school. She and other qualified students were to be sent there by the German government, and she was already looking forward to it. Our stepsister, Helga, was sent to a work farm, and she hated it.

There was a lot of propaganda going on at that time. Leaflets were pasted on stone walls and windows. On the leaflet was a figure dressed all in black with a finger over his mouth and these words written on the bottom, "Shish, the walls have ears." One other thing was a must. We had to hang pictures of Hitler, Himmler, Gobles and Goring on our living room walls.

Otherwise our life was very good, especially the florist business. Money was rolling in faster than we could spend it. My sisters wore a wrap around apron to work and when they came home, they would hang it in the hall closet without emptying their pockets. When Mutti took them down to wash, she emptied the pockets and hundreds of Marks fell out onto the floor. She couldn't believe her eyes. She was outraged when she showed the money to Vati. "Your daughters are so careless with your money. Why isn't this money in the bank where it belongs?"

Vati just smiled. "Oh, there is a lot more where that came from. You can keep the money. Go out and buy yourself something nice."

Mutti looked at him. "You people are all crazy. You should not be so careless with your money. You might need it someday."

Of course, she was right, but as long as we had it, we might as well enjoy it. It was a good thing we did because we lost it all after the war anyway.

Vati looked at her and just shook his head and walked away, and left her standing there with her mouth wide open.

Maria, Gypsy Princess

Workers in the garden in Runn
in the front row left to right Erma, Alma Ida and Gottliebe, Father is above Gottliebe and the overseer is next to him.

We were still without a tub or shower in our home 1943. So every Saturday we all went to a spa to bathe. As many as could fit would pile into our carriage and drive the couple of miles to the spa that spouted hot water constantly. We all showered first, then enjoyed swimming in the hot spring water. A great pastime for the whole family, plus we all got clean.

A villa was vacated when the family living there moved to Tito's area of Yugoslavia. The villa was spacious with roses all around it. The roses were to be sold at the market place. The house and land were there for the taking, and since Father was in the flower business he was told he could take over. Gottliebe and Renate moved out there to take care of the roses and occupy the villa. Alma was happy because she was engaged to Mathias now, so she moved into the apartment Gottliebe and Renate had occupied. That gave her more privacy with Mathias.

The summer wasn't as much fun with Ida and Joseph gone. Alma was preoccupied with Mathias, and soon Vickie would leave for school to become a teacher. I wanted to study ballet in Vienna. I enjoyed dancing, and at first Vati said yes when I asked him if I could go; but then he looked into it more and changed his mind. "Big cities are bombed regularly," he said, its better you stay close to home. I begged and cried and carried on but to no avail. When Father made up his mind that was it, he wouldn't change it. He told me I could always entertain my friends being a tight rope walker instead. How differently my life would have turned out had I been able to go to ballet school.

Maria Reule Woelfl

The Bomb

That long, hot lazy summer I enjoyed my friends, Gretel and Hanelori. We were together when the bomb fell. Our lives were as normal as they could be in wartime, except the air raids. Our stepmother was high strung and when the sirens blared she got very nervous and excited, shouting at us to hurry and get to the cellar. Kurt and I usually obeyed and followed her instructions and stayed in the cellar until the all clear sounded. But when we were not at home, we often didn't obey and stayed outside, squinting into the sun, searching the horizon for incoming planes. We even made bets. Whoever saw the bombers first won, and then we would stand outside and count them. So far our luck had been good, and we were always in a shelter when the bombs hailed down on us. Because we lived in a rural area, we were not bombed as often as the larger cities.

By then Kurt was a tall and lanky eleven-year-old and a troublemaker. He always ran away when he was in trouble. Sometimes he stayed away for hours. He figured the longer he was gone, the less the punishment would be. Sometimes he escaped punishment altogether because his mother would forget all about it.

I was never afraid so I always came home when I was called. I was an eight-year-old with a stubborn streak, but also a sweet disposition. I was a true blue friend and could always be counted upon. My smile could melt anyone's heart, especially my father's.

On this particular day, my best friend Hanelori and I were playing in a grassy ravine behind her house. It was a peaceful place, and many a day we would sit under a tree with a picnic basket listening to the babbling brook and playing with our dolls.

Hanelori was a pretty, petite redhead, her hair braided and woven around her head like a halo. Her skin was very fair, and she had millions of freckles all over her body and beautiful green eyes. She reminded me of an elf. We were sitting in the grass talking, waiting for our friend, Gretel, to show up. Hanelori and I were discussing what we wanted to be when we grew up. She wanted to become a teacher like Mrs. Blummbaum.

"Not me," I said. I thought teaching was boring. I wanted a fun job. I wanted to be a trapeze artist or a ballerina. "Now that's a profession!" I said.

Gretel came down the ravine at that precise moment and asked what we were talking about. "Oh, just what we want to be when we grow up. What do you want to be Gretel?"

"I'll be a great actress someday," she answered, "just like Marlene Dietrich."

Maria, Gypsy Princess

"Yes," I said, "I can visualize you on stage with your gorgeous black hair and beautiful violet eyes. I know you'll knock them dead some day."

A siren blared and we jumped. But then we ignored it and kept talking. We figured it was just another false alarm.

Suddenly there was an unusual whistling and whirring sound that is hard to describe. Like a Fourth of July rocket going off, but instead of going up this one was coming down, and for a split second just before it hit, there was a deadly silence. Then a tremendous boom and we heard glass shattering. We couldn't tell where the bomb had hit, but it sounded very close. Afterwards it was very quiet, except for the siren blaring. The stillness frightened us, and we ran for shelter.

Hanelori's mother ran toward us. "Hurry, hurry!" she yelled, and hustled us into the cellar. Hanelori's father and two brothers were already there when we came down the steps. Needless to say, Hanelori's parents were really angry at us for not coming to the shelter sooner. Gretel clung to me and whispered into my ear, "I'm scared! It sounded like the bomb hit my house. It was so close." As soon as the all clear sounded, we rushed to see what damage the bomb had made. In the street, we saw an unusual sight. There wasn't as much damage as we imagined. The building the bomb hit was almost intact and the bomb's nose was stuck in the top floor of Gretel's house, its tail sticking out the window, aiming towards the sky. When Gretel saw that, she ran screaming towards her house. One of the firefighters standing there caught Gretel, held her fast and wouldn't let her go. She was shouting at him, "But my mother and father are in there?"

"Calm down," he said. "Are you Gretel Graus?"

"Yes!"

"Your mother and father are alright and are looking for you. Now stay here," he ordered. "I'll find them and bring them to you."

She stood holding onto me, shaking all over, waiting for his return.

A lot of commotion was going on with firefighters everywhere, sirens blaring and red lights flashing. People were pouring out of their houses into the street. The firefighters had their hands full holding them back. I was trying to spot my father in the mayhem. He was a volunteer firefighter too and was somewhere in the middle of it all. But too much was going on and in the confusion and disorder, I could not find him.

Police finally blocked off a large area to keep people away from Gretel's house. We all prayed the bomb was a dud and would not go off before they could defuse it. A jeep with three military men drove up. I presumed they were experts in defusing bombs. A high-ranking officer stepped out of the jeep.

"Leute!" People!" he said to the crowd. "I want you to vacate this area immediately. If you live near here, go stay with some relatives or friends. The rest of you go home and stay there until further notice. I am afraid if this bomb goes off before we defuse it, the whole block will be gone. Mach Schnell! Hurry, hurry and disperse."

I spotted my brother, Kurt, in the crowd and wedged myself through the throng to him.

"Mariechen." he said, "What are you doing here?"

"Hanelori, Gretel and I where playing in the ravine when the bomb hit," I said.

"Thank God you're okay. Come on, let's go home. Mutti is probably worried to death and pulling her hair out wondering where we are."

When we got home, Mutti was indeed pacing the floor worrying about us. She was happy to see us home safely and hugged us tight.

Later, when Father came home, he said the bomb was defused and there was very little damage and no serious injuries. We all thanked God. From then on I always listened to Mutti and went to a shelter when the sirens blared. Just another day in the war zone of 1943.

It was quite a job to get that bomb out of the house and a big mess. Gretel's family, the Krause's, had a sweet shop in the bottom part of the house and when this happened, their business was twice as good as before. People wanted to see where the bomb hit. It became a tourist attraction, people coming and going, looking at the house and also buying candy.

****

We didn't know any Jewish people, and if any lived in the area there was no animosity towards them. I didn't find out about the Holocaust until I came to California in 1957 when I worked in a restaurant in Stockton and waited on some Jewish people. I will say they were very demanding. That evening a customer made a derogatory remark about Jews. He called them kinks. I asked why he called them names, and he said, "You should know. You're from Germany where Hitler killed a lot of them."

I said I didn't know what he was talking about.

That's when he told me part of the story of the Holocaust, but I couldn't believe it then.

Chapter 9

We had a heavy snowstorm, and I got sick with a fever and was sniffling, so I had to stay in bed. I was there for days and was going stir-crazy. The fourth day turned out to be nice and sunny, and through the window I watched some of my friends playing in a vacant load cross the street. They were throwing snowballs at each other, laughing and having fun.

I asked Mutti if I could go out too. She said no at first, and I said, "Please," and rolled my eyes, and after the fifth or sixth, "Please," she finally relented and let me go outside. But not until she bundled me up. I had so many clothes on I could hardly walk. Once outside I went a little crazy, scooping up snow as fast as I could, throwing it everywhere and at anyone near me. A truck was coming around the bend, and I was so wild I kept firing one snowball after another. I hit the truck. Then everyone threw snowballs at the truck too. Some hit the windshield, and that made the driver mad. He stopped the truck, stepped out and grabbed the first boy he could, bent him over his knee and paddled his bottom. When he yelped, the man let him loose and was ready to catch another when the window of our house opened and Mutti called me in.

I looked at Eberhard, he wanted to be called Kurt now, and said "Let's go."

He shook his head. "You go. I know what she'll do to us," and he ran away.

I wasn't scared, so I went to the house. Then the front door flew open, Mutti came out, grabbed my arm and held me fast. With her other hand, she hit me as hard as she could across my face. It was a loud slap and my cheek stung and silent tears rolled down my cheek. I couldn't believe she would do such a thing. No one had ever hit me before and the hurt of being slapped was greater than the pain itself.

When she let me go, I was stunned and didn't know what to do next. She did. She shoved me through the door and inside proceeded to undress me, cap, scarf, mittens and so on and while she undressed me she was harping and wailing, "You are so spoiled and deserve more than a slap. If you were my daughter I wouldn't stand for any of your behavior."

I cried quietly, thinking, wait until Father gets home, you'll get yours.

The whole afternoon I sat in a corner of the sofa crying and waiting for Vati and my sister to come home so I could show them what she had done to me. My cheek was red and swollen and you could see her fingerprints on it. I'd been sick for days and now this. It was too much to take.

When Gottliebe came home, she took one look at me and was really angry at Mutti. Mutti, of course, made a big story of it, telling it her way. But my cheek told it better. Gottliebe washed my face in a basin and put something soothing on my cheek. Then she took me to Vati's bedroom and asked what happened. I was hiccupping now, my nose running, and had a hard time getting it all out. She got the gist of the story, had me lie on the bed and stroked my hair. That's how Vati found us. He was angry too and told Mutti it wasn't up to her to punish me or any of his children. After all, she wasn't our mother.

Needless to say, there was a cold front that evening, everyone was quiet, Father at the head of the table and the divided families on either side. No talk, just a lot of glares. I, for one, was glad when dinner was over and we could all go our separate ways.

I didn't want to stay in that house any more. I felt more and more like an outsider. Mutti and her children were stealing my family from me.

A week before Christmas, Ida came home for a few days. She was a Godsend, someone there all the time so I didn't have to be alone with Mutti when I came home from school. Ida told us what a hard time she had delivering her daughter, Inge, in the sanitarium, and baby Inge was still there. She needed to stay a few more weeks to be strong enough to come home. I felt bad for Ida. She had also gained a lot of weight and said it was because in the sanitarium they fed her a lot of rich food such as goose liver and goose fat. Then she proceeded to tell us she was going to Czechoslovakia to visit our sister Emma and her family and meet up with her husband. Because Joseph was in the SS, he couldn't come to Yugoslavia, so Ida decided to go to him and stay with Emma.

That's how I got the idea to go with her to visit Emma and her children, Helmut and Hilde. Emma's husband, Gottlieb, had come home on leave when they first moved to Czechoslovakia and she got pregnant. A girl this time, they named her Hilde. She was almost two years old now.

I asked Ida if she would take me with her. She said only if Vati said I could. So I went to work on Vati. It was a hard sell, but Vati knew how

Maria, Gypsy Princess

unhappy I had been, so he finally gave in, with the stipulation that I would come back before my next birthday, March 8, 1944.

I was looking forward to the trip and seeing Emma, Helmut and meeting my new niece, Hilde. Seeing Joseph again was a plus because he was one of my favorite people. After all, he saved my life the day I almost drowned.

Ida was a different personality then the rest of us Reule girls. Sometimes I thought she didn't belong to our family. Ida's face was oval instead of round and her hair was lighter like mine. The other girls' hair was darker, almost black. I always felt she and I came from a different family. I was blond as a child. Ida was also very quiet and reserved compared to the rest of the clan, a loving and sweet person.

I finally figured out who she resembled, but it was fifty years later when I made the connection. It was our aunt Bertha, father's youngest sister. Ida looked just like her.

Imprint of a Room

Yugoslavia, 1943, a few days before Christmas, Ida and I left on the noon train for Czechoslovakia. The trip would take three days.

I awoke very early the morning of out departure and sat up in bed. I pushed my feet out from under the feather bed cover and stood. There was no heat in the room, and the floor was cold as ice. In my bare feet I ran across to the dresser, turned on the lamp, then put on my slippers. I gazed lovingly at my belongings and all the things in the room. I wanted to form a lasting picture in my mind. I didn't know then that this would be the last time I slept in this room.

In the corner stood a mahogany wardrobe. Carved in the wood were a deer, fawn and hunter with a bow and arrow. The bed Vickie and I shared was the same carved wood and it felt cool and smooth to the touch. A matching dresser, mirror and bench stood on the opposite side of the room.

Above the bed stand was an old cast iron frame with a photo of my paternal grandparents. On the other side where Vickie was still sleeping, a wooden frame carved by my father held a picture of our parents. On the wall over the bed hung a multicolored tapestry my mother had woven years ago. Handmade hooked rugs were spread on the polished wood floor.

I sat on the bench, my fingers moving lightly over a figurine that stood on the dresser, a ballerina in a pink tutu. I turned a key on the bottom and she came to life, twirling around and around to the melody of "The Blue Danube." The ballerina was a gift from my father on my eighth birthday.

Maria Reule Woelfl

I looked at my reflection in the oval mirror and saw two big, velvet brown eyes staring back. I wish I wasn't going, I thought, as I opened a small, carved box on the dresser. The wooden box and the treasures inside were going away gifts from my four sisters, a pair of exquisite silver earrings with blue stones and embroidered handkerchief Ida had made herself a silver five piece German coin from Gottliebe. Multicolored ribbons and two barrettes for my braids from Alma and Vickie. Also a framed photo of the family to take along. Father's gifts were a wool coat and new ski boots.

There were also some presents from the lady who was to become my stepmother and her children, Helga and Kurt. I would miss Kurt. He and I were pals and understood each other. Mutti had robbed me of my family, especially my father, and that hurt deeply. The life I had known was gone forever. Father was preoccupied and so were my sisters. Our mother's illness took her away. Now, a year after her death, Mutti was intruding in our life. I didn't need or want a new mother. We clashed and didn't see eye to eye on anything. She was always bossing me around I couldn't do anything right. I didn't like it

she was not my mother and had no right to discipline me. Any discipline should come from my father or sisters, not her. The main reason I wanted to visit Emma in Czechoslovakia was to get away from Mutti's bossiness.

The presents from my family were early Christmas gifts. I also made each of them a little gift and presented it just before we left for our train. Emotions were running high, everyone hugging and kissing and giving me last minute instruction how to behave and what to do. "Be good, dress warm and mind your sister and don't forget to write." My mind was a whirl, dazed with all the commotion, but when it finally dawned on me I was really leaving, I started to cry. Tears were rolled down my cheeks. Someone took a handkerchief, wiped my eyes and face and held me close. I felt a little better then. As I looking around, my sisters were crying too.

Vati watched the scene for awhile, probably wondering when the commotion would stop. He finally pulled out his pocket watch and announced, "It's time. Put on your hats and coats, and let's go or we'll be late for the train." He opened the front door, took me and Ida by an arm and propelled us out into the crisp wintry day.

I stopped short as I saw the breathtaking view. A blanket of freshly fallen snow covered the yard, and the trees were laden and drooping under the weight of fluffy white. The beauty made an everlasting imprint on my mind. It felt like a special farewell gift from God. The sisters were standing on the steps waving goodbye to us.

As alighted on to the sleigh that stood a few yards from the door, our horse Heidi hitched to it. It was sad to leave, but I was also excited to be taking a long train trip.

I didn't know the journey would last four years. That's how long I was separated from my family. There would be experiences I'd never forget, although I would try.

Farewell at the Station

Vati carried me to the sleigh and put me on the seat. Then he helped Ida up, covered us with a horsehair blanket and sat on the driver's seat. He took the reins, cracked the whip and shouted, "Giddy-up, Heidi, take us to the station."

We arrived in plenty of time and waited on the snow-covered cement. A shrill whistle in the distance announced the train was coming. As it came closer black smoke billowed high into the cold, clear sky. The train's brakes squealed as the engine came slowly to a halt in front of us.

Although it was my idea to visit Emma in Czechoslovakia I now had second thoughts and didn't want to go. "Vati," I said, "Do I have to go?"

"Of course you do, Mariechen. You can't change your mind at this late date. I'm sure once you arrive and get to know your nephew, Helmut, and your niece, Hilde, you'll have a great time."

"But I don't want to go," I pouted, pressing my finger on my lower lip. "I'd rather stay home with you, Vati."

My father was like a God to me. He was my whole world, even more since mother died. I wished Papa would pick me up and hold me close so I could wrap myself in his love and stay there forever. Vati was a handsome man with a ruddy complexion and a black postage stamp mustache. I would compare him to Rhett Butler in *Gone with the Wind*. He looked dashing that day in his black coat with a fur collar and the furry Russian hat he sported on his beautifully shaped head. As I admired him, he bent and picked me up, hugging me tight. His arms felt so good so I snuggled closer and buried my face in his fur collar.

I lifted my head and rubbed my soft cheek against his stubbly one. The scent of his after shave made me sigh. His nearness gave me joy, and tears now flowed freely. Vati kissed my wet cheeks, and then put me on the platform next to Ida. That's when I saw that his eyes were watery too. He wiped my tears. "Come on, Mariechen, stop your crying. As I remember, it was your idea to go visit Emma. Now, be a good girl and mind your sister. Matter of fact, I want you to mind both Ida and Emma while you're there, you hear?"

Chapter 10
The Journey

Ida and I left on the noon train. The porter said we would arrive at our destination the following evening, Christmas Eve, 1943. Our goodbyes were sad, but now we were on the train to Czechoslovakia.

I was upset that morning. So after we settled in, I lay my head on Ida's lap and cried myself to sleep. An hour later I awoke, looked around, slightly confused as to where I was. When I sat up, I found seven other people in our compartment. Ida was by the window on my right, snoozing.

Across from us sat an elderly couple, and next to them a young woman with her son, a Hitler youth. He was about twelve and seemed very proud of his uniform, a blond, blue eyed strapping boy, very fresh and demanding. His mother had green eyes, and her blond braids were wrapped around her head like a crown. She looked like a child herself and had a hard time coping with her son. He wanted to go to the dining car, and she tried to give him some food she had brought along in a basket. He kept refusing. "Nein, Mutti ich bin nicht hunriech lass mich doch inruhe." (Leave me alone, I'm not hungry).

Two German officers were sitting next to me, not paying attention to any of us. One was leafing through some important looking papers and the other reading a newspaper.

The woman across from me was fixing her husband something to eat. From a big basket on her lap, she took a linen napkin, put it on the small table in front of him and asked what he wanted for lunch. "Karl was wilts du haben, ein Worst Brot oder eines mit Kasse? Und vielicht auch ein Bier dazu." ("Do you want a piece of bread with sausage or one with cheese?" "And, how about a beer with that.")

He sat quietly in the corner reading his paper, not saying a word. She took out more and more food, putting it in front of him on the small table. He finally looked up from his paper and said, "Pasta, ich kann doch nicht soviel Essen." (Enough, I can't eat that much.) The woman had big bosoms, red rosy cheeks and a sweet friendly smile. She reminded me of my grandmother.

She asked me if I'd like something to eat too. I looked at Ida for an okay. She was awake now and nodded, yes. The woman said her name was Rosalie and asked mine.

"Mariechen," I said.

"Das is ein shoner name," she answered. (That is a pretty name.) Then she handed me a piece of bread with some Worst on it and told me to enjoy.

I took it and thanked her.

Ida must have gotten hungry too because she stood and took a small bag from the luggage rack and put it on her lap. She took a bottle and two glasses from the bag and poured us some apple cider. Then she fixed herself a slice of bread with cheese and sat back to enjoy it. I was having fun. It was just like a picnic.

While I ate, my eyes wandered around the compartment, and when they fell on the officer sitting next to me, I was startled. He was looking right at me. He smiled and said, "Gutten Tag kleines Freulein woh fahren Sie hin?" (Good day, young lady. What is your destination?)

A little shy, I looked at my sister. She nodded and whispered to tell him.

"Czechoslovakia to visit our sister for Christmas," I answered.

He reached in his pocket and pulled out a chocolate bar and offered it to me. Chocolate, I thought it was hard to come by in wartime. It sure looked good. Again I looked at Ida, and she nodded. I took the chocolate bar and thanked him.

The other officer next to him said, "Come, Franz, let's you and I go to the dining car. Watching these good people eat is making me hungry too. They stood, clicked their heels together and left.

The disagreement was still going on between the boy and his mother. She was trying to hand him a slice of bread with liverwurst and he still kept refusing it, "Nein Mutti ich mage das doch nicht." (No Mutti, I don't like that. I want to go to the dining car to eat.) His mother kept telling him, "Nein, nein, it is too expensive." He told her he didn't care, he had money his father had sent him, and he could spend it any way he wanted. His mother pleaded with him to eat, but he just shook his head and didn't accept anything.

"Aber Liebling, that money is for your birthday, to buy a bicycle, not spend for food." He didn't like the liverwurst. He just shook his head and pouted. She finally gave up, ignored him completely and enjoyed her own bread with liverwurst.

The boy she called Hans must have gotten hungry because when I looked later he was eating a slice of bread with cheese and drinking something from

Maria Reule Woelfl

a bottle. His mother was smiling and cooing and whispering into his ear. He was still pouting and shook his head to whatever she offered.

Ida and I were on the train overnight and late into the next day. To get to Czechoslovakia we had to travel the width of Austria, bypassing Wien. (Vienna,) The town of Japonica where my sister Emma lived was on the Austrian border. Our arrival time was supposed to be 3:00 p.m. Christmas Eve day, but we didn't arrive until 5:00. The station was locked, and no one was in sight. We stood on the platform wondering if we were forgotten. It was cold and getting dark, and no one came to pick us up.

We stood there about twenty minutes not knowing what to do next. Should we wait here or start walking and hope we found a house close by. Emma wouldn't forget to pick us up. She must not have received our telegram. It looked bleak. We would have to walk for miles. We couldn't even see any lights in the distance. It was now 5:30 on Christmas Eve and we had to walk or sit around and freeze. We were thankful it was a clear night and the road was cleared of snow.

Ida put the rucksack on my back, handed me the overnight case, picked up the two larger pieces of luggage, and we started towards town. We walked about a half-hour and there still was no light ahead, only darkness. We were blessed with stars so we could at least see where we were going. We were getting tired so we stopped and sat on the suitcases to rest awhile, and then went on. In another twenty minutes or so we finally saw a light in the distance, which turned out to be a house. We stopped and knocked on the door.

"Who is it?" a woman said, and we were in luck, it was in German.

Ida told her who we were and that we just walked from the train station.

The door opened quickly, and Frau Muller bade us come into the kitchen to get warm. She made us some hot chocolate, set an assortment of baked goods in front of us and urged us to eat and drink.

She left to ask her husband what they could do for us. Herr Muller came and told us he sent his field hand to saddle a horse and ride to town and get someone to come pick us up. We knew it would take him awhile so we took our coats off and sat back to enjoy their hospitality. We felt badly because we were holding the Muller's back from celebrating Christmas Eve.

But they told us they would be celebrating Christmas Day when their children arrived. An hour later Joseph showed up in automobile. We were so happy to see Joseph. Especially Ida! She hadn't seen her husband for over a year. They hugged and gave each other a shy kiss. We said good-bye to the Muller's, and Joseph tried to give some money for the young man who came to get him. They shook their heads, "Nein, nein as ist nicht notwendig," but

Joseph put the money into her hand when he shook it. Ida sat in front and I settled into the back seat and almost fell asleep on the way to Emma's.

When we arrived, the door flew open and Emma ran and opened the back door and pulled me out, hugging me. She said how sorry she was no one was there to pick us up. "We received your letter that you were coming, but not your telegram. We didn't know what time you'd arrive. I'm so glad you're here," and she hustled us into the house.

Helmut was a little over three years old now and Hilde would be two in April. They were both asleep. The Christmas tree was lit and the table set for dinner. I was glad because I was starving. I don't remember exactly what we ate, only it was good and I was happy to be there and in a warm place. I was so tired I didn't even care if Saint Nick had left me a present or not. All I wanted was a bed and a pillow to lay my head on and sleep for a week.

The next morning I was still tired, but since I was sleeping in the same bed with Emma and Helmut, it was impossible to sleep late. Emma got up to take care of Hilde and start the fire in the stove to fix breakfast. Helmut was crawling all over me, saying, "Get up, Christmas is here." I tried to turn over and push him away, but it was no use. He kept shaking me "Aufstehen Ria," and when I wouldn't respond, he crawled over me and tried to open my eyes with his fingers.

"Ria, Ria, get up." He couldn't say Maria so Ria I was for the time being. I finally relented and sat up.

Just then Emma came back with Hilde in her arms. "Are you up?"

"Ja, how can I sleep with Helmut haunting me?"

She just laughed, "Ja, no one can sleep after he is awake. Come into the kitchen and have some hot milk and talk to me while I fix breakfast."

She asked about Vati, the sisters and our mother's death. I had to relive it for her and my eyes got misty. She saw me getting sad. "You know," she said, "Saint Nick left you a present." My eyes lit. "Wait until Ida and Joseph get up."

"No. I can't wait that long. They might sleep in. Please."

"Well, okay, go look in the hall closet."

I jumped off the chair and ran to the hall. My eyes opened wide. Just what I longed for, new skis to go with the new boots Vati gave me. I grabbed them and ran back to the kitchen. "Thanks. Can I go try them out now?"

"Don't you think you should get dressed first?" she laughed.

"Oh, ja." I ran back and pulled on the clothes I had worn the night before. Emma tried to get me to wait, but I was anxious to go outside. Just then Ida and Joseph came out of their room and I ran right into them.

"Hold it, where are you off to?"

I just held up my skis and kept going. Outside, I sat on the steps to put the skis on but couldn't handle them by myself. So I went back in to ask Joseph to help.

"Not until after breakfast," he said.

I had to relent and wait. I was glad because I really was hungry and everything tasted good. When we were finished with breakfast, it was time to try out my new sled! Helmut wanted to go out too, so Joseph brought the sled around and helped me with the skis. He stood me up, held my hand, steadying me, and with his other hand pulled Helmut on the sled. I kept falling down, and it took me a few days to be able to stand and walk with skis on.

Ida and Inge as a baby

A few days later, Ida and Joseph went to get Inge from the hospital. They were gone two days, and when they came back the house was noisy and crowded again, but it was a happy time for all of us. Joseph's leave was up and he had to get back to the war. It was so peaceful in the little town of Japonica. We forgot there was a war for awhile.

It wasn't easy for two women to care for four children and all the other work that had to be done on a farm. I was eight years old and I was a lot of help although it was difficult some time going to a new school and then take care of three children afterward. It didn't give much time to making new

Maria, Gypsy Princess

friends. I was lucky because other were many German families lived in the same area and most of them were our relatives.

Emma's in-laws lived in the same village, and our Uncle William Schelske and his family were a few miles away in another village. I was happy to have some family to visit. The skis came in handy too, since I had three miles to get to school and the same back. It was easier than walking.

We hadn't heard a thing from Runn in awhile. The mail was getting slower and slower. Only one letter and a birthday card in the time span of two months and I was getting scared. Would I ever get home again? I turned nine March 8, came and went so quick and I was still in Czechoslovakia with no way to get home.

Vickie wrote to Emma, and informed us that Mutti and Vati, Alma and Mathias would have a double wedding in June 19, 1944.

*Weddings Mutti, Vati and Alma and Mathias
Eberhard on left and Gottliebe above Vati and Mathias.*

Easter was near and Emma made me a beautiful Easter outfit. We all had Easter baskets, and the kids were very excited waiting for the bunny to come. They enjoyed all their goodies, and so did I. Hilde turned two in late April. When she ate her cake, she had more on her face than in her mouth; it was fun for all of us watching her eat. She was a happy child, not like Inge. Poor Inge was always sickly and cried a lot.

Maria Reule Woelfl

Time passed with no news from my father, Joseph or Gottlieb. It was like we were on a desert island. We kept hearing bad news that the German Army was getting the worst of it and was driven back, and the enemy was coming closer and closer. It looked like the war was almost over, and the Germans were losing. The propaganda on the radio played it down, so we weren't sure what to believe. Ida and Emma were really worried for their husbands, but there was no way to find out where they were or how they were doing.

At the time, a new hairstyle came out, and I wanted the new do. I'd been wearing my hair parted in the middle with pigtails hanging down my back last year I had short hair when I came for my visit. The new style was a roll on top of the head, then pulled down and back into braids. Emma told me I couldn't wear it like that. I wouldn't listen and had a friend help me make the new style. When I came home, I was scared to go inside. Emma saw me in the yard and called me to come in. She was really angry with me for changing my hair. She tried to take it down. I ran, but she caught me and pulled the top of my hair apart. I was screaming and trying to get away from her again. She grabbed my arm, put me over her knee and paddled my behind. I kept screaming and howling, and she kept saying, "Will you mind me, now?"

I said, "No, I will not, you can't make me."

She told me to go sit in the milk shed until I cooled off. I was there until supper time, crying, but I wouldn't give in. The next day she caved in and let me wear it my way. I told her I was sorry for being bad and all was forgiven. Until the next time, that is.

It was Spring and the work went on. There were cows to be milked, stock to be fed, and land to be plowed. Wheat, flax and rye were to be sown as well and potatoes were to be planted. The household chores wouldn't stand still either. Inge turned a year old in June and seemed better, but she liked to be held and sung to, so I did that as often as I could. Ida was so busy with all the other work she couldn't spend enough quality time with Inge, and that made her sad. She was really pleased and grateful I could spend so much time with her baby and told me so.

Emma's house and property was in the middle of town and connected to the neighbor's property. To have attached properties was the norm in those days. On the side of the house was a big gate with a small door to walk through. It was a completely enclosed courtyard with the barn on one end. Behind the barn was a vegetable garden and fruit trees. The gate could be opened so you could drive the horse and wagon through. The fields were in surrounding areas, but most farmers lived in town.

The war raged on, and we heard more and more disturbing news that the German army was losing. That scared us because we had heard how cruel the Russians were. We were told that when they took over a village they molested the women and children. The men weren't safe either. We were frightened of the invasion of the Russians. We were told they showed no mercy towards their enemies.

Ida and Emma still hadn't heard from their husbands and no news from Yugoslavia, so our lives went on. Finally, summer was here and school was out. Everything went smoothly now because everybody was working together and helping each other out. Emma's in-laws had taken care of the children while I was in school, but now they had to catch up with their own work. I was stuck and had to care of the children all the time instead just after school. There also was a swimming hole we used a lot. Although I was scared of water and stayed in the shallow end, it was fun. Everyone teased me about it, but I didn't care. I stayed in my shallow water and told them I was just fine there.

In the fall came hog killing time, same as in Rumania, everyone working at cutting the pig up and utilizing all the different parts. I had finally made friends, so once in awhile I could go out and play with them. It was fun just to be free and not take care of children all the time. We played hide and seek or touch ball and told ghost stories. We just ran free without a care and it was wonderful, I was just fine. Summer passed into fall, and there was even more work to be done, harvesting and preparing for the long winter. This season sent my sisters out to the fields for long hours even into the night. They had to cut grass to make hay, thresh and haul hay and straw into the barn, then get it up to the hayloft. They took the wheat and rye to the mill to make flour. Always more and more work to do. I helped wherever I was needed. Living on the farm was simple, we had good food and love. The hard work and longs made one forget some time there was a war on.

Maria Reule Woelfl

Mutti, Vati, Eberhard and the driver, with the family in the background in Runn

We finally another letter came from Yugoslavia. My sister, Vickie, wrote that everything was unsure. Tito and his partisans were taking more and more territory back from the Germans and were driving the German army back. It wasn't looking good for the German families who had settled in Yugoslavia on Hitter's orders. Vati had sent Mutti and Kurt to Austria. Mutti was with child and they were afraid if they had to flee, she wouldn't be able to walk far and might go into premature labor. That was the last letter we received from Runn, none from Joseph or Gottlieb. We spent another winter and spring in Japonica. In April we ended up having to flee on a covered wagon drawn by two horses, to East Germany. It took us a month to get there.

Chapter 11
Marichen Fleeing

We left early in the morning, April 19, 1945 and traveled towards Germany. We were fleeing from the Russian army that was ascending on us. Our aim was to be sure we ended up in the British or American sector and not the Russians.

Twenty wagons left Japonica. Everyone had been preparing extra food to take with us, and it was loaded into the wagons. The heavy stuff went in the bottom of the hull. Clothes and bedding were put on top to sleep on. Pots, pans, lanterns and all kind of things we needed for making a fire and cooking were hung on the side of the wagon or stowed under the driver's seat. After a few days we encountered some heavy vehicles in the middle of the road, abandoned by the German army. Soldiers were also fleeing on foot. They looked bedraggled; many didn't even have shoes to wear. Their feet were wrapped in newspaper or whatever they could find. Those who still had shoes the soles were flopping, making it almost impossible to walk. It was slow going for them. They looked defeated, some were wounded and hungry, but they kept walking. It was a sad sight, and we felt sorry for them and gave them food, water and also shoes. Wives' whose husbands were in the war gave soldiers some of their husbands' belongings. They hoped and prayed some kind person would do the same for their husbands or sons.

One evening we stopped near a village and asked the farmers if we could use their barns to sleep in, also if we could get some water from their wells. They were kind enough to let us stay. A lot of the older children my age and up slept in hay lofts around the area. When we stopped in the evening we'd circle the wagons just as they did in the old West. We had to find stones and firewood to cook our meals. It wasn't an easy task getting things going, especially with the young children hungry and crying and the older ones running around driving everyone crazy. I, for one, didn't have time to play or run wild because I had to hunt for firewood and gather stones. Emma and Ida had their hands full with the three kids, building a fire then preparing food.

Of course, everyone was in the same fix, and we all had to do what we must to survive. The men hauled water for their families and looked after the horses. Some of the women offered to milk the cows for the farmers so we could have fresh milk for the little ones. The farmer's wives were usually happy to let them. They gave us fresh milk and sometimes eggs, also a hen or two. In return, we gave them some of our clothes. They really appreciated that. All in all, it worked out for everybody. After the first few days things went smoother. By then everyone knew their job and the routine.

One morning we had a late start and were way behind the other wagons. It was slow going, one of our horses named Franz was lazy, and so all the hard pulling fell on Gretchen. She was a good worker while lazy Franz just walked along side not pulling much. It was hard for Gretchen, and she was getting tired of it. But there was nothing to be done with a lazy horse because no one wanted to trade for Franz. So we fell way behind the other wagons.

On that day we came upon a burning truck left in the middle of the road. Emma was driving, and she took a slow wide berth around the burning truck, but our wagon came too close to the edge of the road. The horses spooked and the whole wagon, with Inge and Hilde in it, flipped sideways into a ravine. Most of our belongings fell on top of the two kids. Emma had her hands full keeping the horses in line. Ida, Helmut and I had been walking behind the wagon. As soon it went over we made a beeline down to the wagon to dig the girls out. We heard them crying, but it took awhile to find them. They were lucky nothing heavy fell on them. Emma was also fortunate she and the horses didn't flip upside into the ravine too. She really had her hands full getting the horses under control. We thanked God no one was hurt or killed that day.

We were also fortunate that two other wagons were behind us and came to our rescue. A strong, young lad, his grandfather and two women helped us with the wagon. It took all of us working together more than an hour to turn the wagon right side up again. Then we still had to put everything back into the hull, before we could move on. The ravine was too deep where we went over, so we had to drive quite a while until we came to a place where the wagon could be driven up onto the road again.

The other wagons were way ahead of us by then. When we hadn't shown up for an hour or so, they got worried and finally sent two riders back to see if we were all right. When the found us it took over an hour, to get to our appointed station. They didn't know we were in trouble and we didn't catch up to them until they stopped for the evening. Even then they didn't realize we were so many miles behind. The rest of the troop had already started their fires and were cooking their food when we couth up with them. They thought of us and cooked enough for us too. The men came and helped us get everything in order in the wagon and the women fed us. I, for one, was glad because I didn't have to go find stones and firewood for the evening meal. I still had to get it set up for breakfast, though.

Always the same routine, in the morning breakfast, then put everything back in the wagon and move on. "It was a whole month of stopping for the night, packing everything up after breakfast, and then back on the road again.

As we traveled along, we would hear stories from time to time on news of the war also some gruesome tales from a man who escaped the Russian army. He told us they were fleeing on foot when the Russians came upon them. They drove them like cattle to a secluded place and made them dig a grave. He told us they made them line up in a row in front of the hole and shot them down, including women and children. When they fell into the hole the screams were piercing. He continued on saying that they fell into their grave, landing on top of each other, the ones still alive buried under the dead bodies. The few who were spared had to cover the others up with dirt. When the men who were spared in order to cover the bodies heard the screams coming from the grave, some jumped after them to dig them back out, but they were shot for their efforts. The rest still alive did what they were told and covered all the bodies, listening to the screams of their loved ones as they shoveled dirt onto them.

The man who told us the story had escaped one night when the Russians were so drunk most of them had passed out. The poor man. He lived to tell the tale, but had paid a huge price for living. He had to endure that horror the rest of his life. His wife and son were shot and buried in the hole he helped cover up. Now he had to live seeing that awful sight in his dreams as he goes on with his life. Also hearing the screams in his mind and seeing his family fall into that hole, powerless to help them. He had to live with his pain and wander aimlessly around the ruins of his country without his family. We sympathized with him but were relieved we hadn't encountered the same brutal enemy on our journey.

****

When we came upon a river it was always a relief because they would stop a little early and let the children go swimming. Even the horses were happy to be able to go in the water and get a good scraping and take a swim. The men and boys would go fishing and we'd have fried trout for dinner. Also the adults would take baths and wash clothes. The women would go to a secluded place, strip down to their underwear and wash their clothes and themselves at the same time. Washing their hair was a more difficult task, but the women did it while they took their baths then rinsed it with white vinegar. Their hair came out clean and shiny. Going to the bathroom was also a tricky job. Either we ran behind a bush and peed or did like some the older women did. They wore long dresses and no undergarment and while walking they just went to the side of the road, spread their legs, lifted their skirts a bit and just let it flow. When they were finished they got back in line and walked on.

We were hoping and praying to get to a British or American sector instead of the Russians. We were all elated the day we finally spied the German border and saw the occupying forces were British. It was a happy occasion for all, but especially the children. They ran towards them with out stretched arms. The British soldiers didn't know what to make of us, so they held their hands up and shouted "Halt!" We all stopped, scared to move. My uncle, William, was in the lead wagon so he got down and held his hands up with his papers in them. He walked slowly towards the guards and, when he was a few feet away, he stopped. He told them in German who we were and that we wanted to cross the border into Germany. The guard held his hand up again and told him in German to stay where he was. Then he went to call army headquarters to find out what to do with us.

When he came back, he motioned my uncle closer so he could look at his papers. The soldier told him in German it was okay to go on. We older children got our courage back and moved slowly towards them. Some other soldiers disappeared into a little hut at the border and returned with chocolate bars in their hands. They motioned us closer and handed us the chocolates, gesturing to divide them between us. That made us smile. We thanked them and ran back to our wagons to show off our goodies.

They lifted the checkpoint bar and waved us through. We drove a few more kilometers until we came upon a village. We stopped on the outskirts while some of the men went to check the town out. They came back within an hour to tell us what they found. It was late now, and the last night we would sleep in our wagons. The next day they found lodging for most of us in the town of Whimsies. We moved into a room in the schoolhouse. There wasn't enough room for everybody so others moved on to another village where they were housed in barracks. We were elated that the British army was in the area. Little did we know the Brits would move on in a few days, and the Russian army would take over the town.

In traveling for more than a month, fleeing the Russians to get to Germany it was not enough, because we still faced the beast. Moving on again was not an option, because we had nowhere to go.

Chapter 12
Germany summer and fall of 1945

Our family wasn't the only one placed in the schoolhouse, a family Kreuter also stayed there. Frau Kreuter's husband had been in the German army, and it was a miracle they had found each other so soon. They and their three children, a boy and two girls, were now living in a room on the second floor of the schoolhouse. As I remember, Herr Kreuter was in the S.S. and therefore, in hiding.

The day the Russians took over the town came too soon for us. We didn't have enough time to get settled before that horrendous night, and one of the longest we ever experienced. A night I'll never forget.

We knew how villainous and cruel the Russian soldiers were towards the German people. They hated us and wanted to wipe us all out. Now that the war was over, they took out their hate on women and children. We were scared they would find us. My sisters hung blankets and sheets over the windows so light wouldn't be seen from outside. We had a cold supper so smoke from the chimney or the smell of cooking wouldn't be detected.

What the soldiers did to women and children was well known and enough to make hair stand on end all over your body. Scared isn't the right word. We were terrified. It was my fault they found us. I got nosy and lifted a corner of the blanket to peek out a window. I couldn't see a thing, it was too dark outside, with my bad luck, just as I lifted the blanket three Russian soldiers were passing the school. The schoolhouse had no electricity, but they saw the light from our kerosene lamp.

The soldiers immediately came up the steps and pounded on the front door. We were scared to open it. The pounding became fiercer, so finally Emma opened the door a tiny bit and asked what they wanted. They didn't answer but pushed her aside and forced themselves into the hallway.

Just then Frau Kreuter, the lady who lived upstairs came halfway down the stairway to see what the commotion was about. When she saw the soldiers, she turned and quickly ran back. She had to warn her husband so he could hide. If the Russians found him they would shoot him on the spot or send him to a Russian prison.

The soldiers tried to push themselves into our room, but Ida came out with Inge in her arms and whispered, "Let's go up stairs to visit with Frau Kreuter."

The soldiers were drunk and smelled of sour mash and sweat. One looked just like pictures I'd seen of Cossacks. He had a matted, stringy beard and looked like he hadn't washed or bathed for months. They had rotten teeth and bad breath, dirty clothes and muddy boots. All three stank to high heaven. We were repulsed by them, but there wasn't anything we could do about it.

Emma lifted Hilde into her arms, took Helmut's hand and headed upstairs. I closed the door to our room and followed close behind, looking over my shoulders to see what the Russians were up to. They were weaving from side to side, bumping into each other, but they were following us up the stairs. I passed Emma and Ida to tell Frau Kreuter we were coming. When I came into the entry hall, Herr Kreuter was nowhere to be seen. Their children were all on the bed, the two older ones still awake. I whispered, "Is everything okay, Frau Kreuter.

She just nodded and whispered, "Yes." I could see the terror in her eyes.

Their place had a small hallway with a sofa, chair and a small, square table. They must have just finished their evening meal because dishes and food were still on the table. I went and started helping her put the food away, and that's when the door burst open. One Russian pushed Emma in front of him and another was pulling Ida behind him.

Ida held her daughter Inge, and he pointed to Inge, then to the crib, saying something none of us could understand. Apparently he wanted Ida to put Inge in the crib. Ida shook her head, "I have to feed," she said in German.

The soldier didn't like that at all. He pulled Inge away and threw her into the crib. Inge started to wail. Ida tried to pick her up, but he stopped her. Then he grabbed Ida and tried to kiss her. She fought, struggling to free herself from his grasp. That made him angrier. He shoved her, trying to get her out the door so he'd have her alone. We screamed and came to her rescue, pulling her back inside. He shoved us and grabbed her again. Another soldier grabbed Emma, yanked her onto the sofa, trying to kiss her neck, his hands all over her. She screamed. We had never heard such fear in her voice. She tried to get free, but he held her, his other hand reaching under her dress. She slapped his hand hard and pulled away.

Maria, Gypsy Princess

We children tried to help her. We opened a window and screamed. The third soldier went after Frau Kreuter. He cornered her, tried to rip her blouse off, pulling her toward the bed where her children where lying, her youngest screaming now, too. Twisting from his grasp, she picked up her daughter, rocking her, humming and trying to put her back to sleep. The Russian pulled the child away, tossed her back on the bed and she started screaming again. We left Emma and rushed to help Bertha. Then we kept hollering out of the open window for help.

"Hielfe, hielfe!" But of course no one was close enough to hear. The tug of war went on for what seemed like hours. Finally, Emma told me to go downstairs, run to the village for help. They were fighting for their virtue, and Frau Kreuter was scared for her husband, also the children. The soldiers were already very drunk. So the women stopped fighting and poured them homemade wine. They pretended to join them, watering down their own drinks. If they could get the soldiers even more drunk, they would pass out. Emma pulled me a side and told me to go to the village the get a Russian interpreter and bring him back to talk to the soldiers so they would leave. I put a dark coat and headed out. Now I was really, really scared, going out into the dark streets and through a village I were I didn't know anyone. All the people were strangers to me, and I was scared I might run into more Russians. It was so dark I couldn't see my hand before my eyes.

I walked slowly down the dirt road. I needed to run but I had to walk and stay close to wall so I wouldn't get lost. I felt sure I would die that night. But I made myself put one foot in front of the other, one step at a time. I hesitated now and then, listening if someone was coming. As I got closer to the village, I could see light in some houses, and went to the first one, then stopped, afraid to approach and knock on the door.

My hand shook as fear took over. I couldn't let it stop me. I had to do this to save my sisters and Frau Kreuter. I don't know where my courage came from, but I finally knocked on the door, terrified a Russian soldier would answer. There was a lot of noise inside, and at first they didn't hear so I pounded my fist on the door again.

Finally a woman came to the door. "Ja, was wollen Sie haben? Warum lauffen, Sie so spatt aleine drausen herum?" "(What to you want? Why are you out so late, all by yourself?)"

Stuttering, I forced myself to tell her what was happening and asked if someone could help us.

She shook her head. "We need help ourselves. There is no help tonight!"
"I'm looking for the Russian Interpreter, I said, "is he here?"
"Nein," she said Er ist nicht hir!" "(He is not here!)"
"Danke!" "Thanks!"

I walked on to the next house and the next. I must have knocked on every door in the village and went through the same spiel over and over. There was no hope. I couldn't find the interpreter, German or Russian. When I came to the last house, I was so tired I could hardly move. I knocked loudly. A Russian soldier came to the door and said in good German, "What to you want?"

I told him we needed him to come and get rid of three soldiers bothering my sisters. The interpreter looked at me like I was mad. Then he grinned, shook his head and laughed out loud.

"I'll come in the morning when I am finished here," he said. I'm busy with my own Freuleins so go back and get some sleep. You shouldn't be out so late, something might happen to you." He slammed the door in my face and went back to what he was doing, molesting the woman of that house.

I crept quietly back to the schoolhouse. I was scared to go. I knew Emma would be really angry and blame me because I had peeked out the window earlier. When I went in, the Russians were still there, but in drunken stupors. One was hanging onto Bertha with a steel grip, slobbering all over her. Another was on the sofa snoring, the third nuzzling Emma's neck. When she saw me, she jumped up, knocking his head back. He grabbed for her hand, but she got away and ran to me, hoping I had good news. Ida was nowhere in sight.

Emma looked at me with longing. I felt sad to tell her no one was coming to rescue us. When I turned my head, Bertha and Ida were standing behind us, their eyes sad and exhausted. The sun was coming up. The Russians must've gotten tired. They stood and came over and kissed the women hard on their mouths, while each struggled to get away. Then, just as suddenly, the soldiers let go, pinched their butts and staggered out. In a moment I followed to see if they were really leaving. One stumbled and almost fell down the step. They were cursing, and I was sure it was vulgar. The voices sounded ugly. When the front door slammed shut, I let out a breath of relief.

I know you must wonder why they didn't rape the women. I don't know, unless they were too drunk. All I can say is thank God they didn't!

It was early in the morning now and we were struggling to stay awake. After the soldiers left we waited awhile to make sure they would not come back. Then Frau Kreuter called to her husband. "Hans, are you alright?" She lifted an edge of the mattress; "Komm raus, Hans, die sind jetzt weg." (Come out, Hans, they are gone now). When Herr Kreuter crawled out he couldn't stand at first. He was so shaken he looked gray. His wife helped him sit on the bed. He put his hands to his face and sobbed. Bertha put her arms around him, saying, "Liebling, I am sorry." He removed his hands and looked haggard, ten years older. His hair was almost white, which I hadn't noticed before. Hiding under the mattress all night must have aged him.

It was horrible for all of us but think what it must have cost Hans Kreuter to lie under the mattress listening to the women's cries and one of them his wife. If he had come to their rescue, as an SS officer he would have been shot on sight or taken away to and sent to a Russian prison in Siberia. How horrible that would have been for the children. Especially his children, it would have broken their hearts.

It had been a long night, and we were all exhausted. We went back to our own room and Emma fixed a cold breakfast, cheese, bread, worst, milk for the children and tea for us. Ida fed Inge while she ate some bread and cheese, then she took off her shoes and dress, curled up on the bed with her daughter and was fast asleep before we even started to eat.

None of us ate much. All we wanted was to sleep for days. I snuggled up in my warm feather bed, and as soon as I hit the pillow fell into a deep sleep. I had horrible nightmares, dreaming I was little again and big, hungry dogs were chasing me. Suddenly the dream took another direction, and I was back on the wagon train and needed to go to the bathroom, but there was nowhere to go. That dream awoke me just long enough to get out of bed, pull out the chamber pot, and pee. I crawled back under the feather bed and dreamt on. This time I was running and fighting to get away from Russian soldiers, my legs felt like lead, I couldn't make them work. The Russians getting closer and closer, I kept running and crying. "Mama, help me, help me Mama!"

Ida came and shook me. "Mariechen wake up, you're having a nightmare. Wake up, you're okay."

When I awoke, tears were rolling down my cheeks. I sat up and took a minute to realize where I was. When I smelled food cooking, I knew I was safe, and as always, I was hungry, my stomach growling. "Oh, Ida, I had the most horrible dreams. I'm glad you woke me up." All the others were already up. Emma was by the stove, cooking.

"Come on, Mariechen," Ida said, "help me set the table." She didn't have to tell me twice. I jumped out of bed, hurried to the basin and washed my face and hands. Since I had messed up last night lifting the blanket, I tried to stay away from Emma. I was scared, I had felt her hand across my face many times in the last two years so I took a wide berth from Emma's reach. I shrunk inside of me.

Emma didn't say anything. She just handed me dishes to put on the table. After we all sat down to eat, Emma said, "Maria, why don't you say grace today."

"God, thank you for keeping us from harm last night, and please keep us safe from now on, also in our future travels. Bless us. We are grateful for the food we are about to eat. Thank you. Amen."

We ate in silence. We were all in our own thoughts. You could feel tension in the air. The silence was broken when Helmut teased Hilde, and she started to cry. Emma slapped his hand, "If you don't behave, you'll have to stand in the corner without breakfast." He pouted a while but when no one paid attention to him, he decided to eat.

I was waiting for Emma to say something to me and was surprised she hadn't. I was afraid she was fuming inside, and I would really get it later. After the meal, Ida and I did the dishes and put everything away. I asked Emma if I could go sit in the garden and get some fresh air for a while.

"Yes," she said, "but you have to take Helmut and Hilde with you."

I was only scared of the Russians but Emma too and didn't dare say anything to her. I took a little wagon from the corner, and Helmut held the door open so I could take it outside. I put Hilde in, took Helmut's hand and started down the street. We didn't go far. I didn't want to run into Russian soldiers so I turned back. When Emma saw us she asked, "Why are you back so soon?"

I didn't know what to tell her so I stuttered a little. "Helmut… ah… has to go to the bathroom."

"Go take him, then I want to talk to you."

Oh, here it comes, I thought. I'm really going to get it now. When Helmut and I came back Emma was sitting on my bunk bed, knitting. She told the kids to go play and asked me to sit next to her. I must've looked scared because she said, "I'm not going to hit you. I just want to tell you how proud of you I was last night. I know you were scared, but you walked through the whole village in the dark looking for help and found the interpreter. I know he refused come but you did everything you could to help us. I'm also proud how you handled yourself. You did really well fighting the Russians off. You were a great help to all of us. Thank you!"

Now I must have looked stunned, because she went on. "I know you thought I would be angry because you looked out the window last night, but I thought about it and realized they would have come anyway. Maybe they'll leave us alone now and I'm glad it's over. Let's pray they don't come back."

I was flabbergasted to hear such praise from Emma. It was unheard of, and I didn't know how to respond. So I didn't say anything. I just sat there and let the tears roll down my cheeks. It was a late reaction to all that had happened in the last few hours, not to mention the last few years. Emma put her arms around me, held me tight and rocked me slowly in her arms as if I was her child. What a wonderful sister.

The next few days were uneventful. I hadn't seen any soldiers since that night but stayed close to home anyway. None of us wanted to talk about what had happened, so we kept our fear and feelings inside. The Russians must have behaved badly because they were celebrating their victory. They won another battle. As a gift, their allies gave them a part of Germany.

School was out for the summer. Of course, that didn't matter to me. I had missed so much school it would take me forever to catch up. I'd had little time for myself, but knew it wouldn't last long because Emma and Ida were looking for jobs and as soon as they found them, I'd be busy taking care of the children again. We weren't planning to stay too long in this village anyway. Emma and her in-laws and some of the other families made a decision they decided to go back to Rumania soon as we could. So my education was short lived, because I wouldn't be able to go to school in Rumania. I would have a hard time catching up with my schooling if ever.

A few days later I was holding Inge on my lap feeding her. When I looked up, Ida was watching me intently. When I asked her why, she said, "I've been watching you the last twenty minutes, and you've been scratching your head constantly. What's going on?"

I told her my head had been itching for over a week now and was getting worse. She came over, parted my hair and looked at my scalp.

"Oh, my God, Maria, your head is full of lice!" She took Inge from me put her down on the floor. "Let's wash your hair right of way, she said when Emma comes home she'll know what to do."

Indeed Emma knew what to do. She took out a very fine comb, laid a black shawl on the table and had me bend over it. Then she started to comb my hair. As soon as that comb went through my hair, I saw little white bugs crawling on the black cloth. Emma picked each one up and cracked it between her thumbnails. The little buggers were very hard to kill. While we were busy doing that, there was a knock on the door. Emma didn't know what to do. She really didn't want anyone to know I had lice. It was Frau Kreuter wanting to borrow something. Ida opened the door slightly and tried to keep her from entering. She came around Ida, and her eyes opened wide when she saw what Emma was doing.

"Oh!" she said, "I see you're busy. I'll come back later." She turned on her heels and walked out.

Emma kept on with her job, and after she combed out as many lice as she could, she took me and bent my head over the sink. She unscrewed the top of the kerosene lamp, poured some of the liquid on her hand and rubbed it into my scalp. She then tied the black shawl tightly around my head. As soon as scarf was in place, the lice were having dance fest some were doing the jig and others the polka! I thought I was going mad, and the smell was horrid. I looked for a clothespin to put on my nose. Emma said, "I know it's awful, but if you don't keep the stuff on at least two hours, you'll never get rid of them." I suffered with the itching for days and we had to do it over again to get rite of the little buggers. I stayed close to home, reading and telling the kids fairy tales. When I finally was able to go out, Bertha's daughter Ermgard asked me if I would like to play with her and some friends. I was eager to do something different, especially with someone more my age for a change, so I agreed to play hairdresser with them.

A small storage shed was in the back of schoolhouse, and that's where we went to play. There were four of us, two boys and two girls and they all brought combs, brushes and towels. Inside the shed Ermgard told me to sit on a bench. She draped a towel around me. The other girl, Rose, started to undo my braids, and a boy named Karl came over with his comb and parted my hair and looked at my scalp intently. I asked why I was the only one being the client.

"Oh we'll take turns," said Ermgard. She and a boy named Jorgen sat on each side of me and looked at my scalp with great interest. Then it dawned on me what they were up to. They were looking for lice. That made me angry, and I pushed both of them away, stood and ran out, my eyes stinging with tears. My life sure wasn't easy when I was younger, but in the last few years it had worsened, and now lice! Why didn't anybody else get lice? It wasn't fair. Why did everything bad happen to me? Having to leave our home in Rumania when I was five, then Austria and Yugoslavia and Czechoslovakia, now to move back to Rumania again. Living in a different country every few years wasn't any fun. My mother dying when I was only seven left a big void in me, and it felt like I had been alone ever since. Then to top it all off, my father brings strangers into our home and tells me this woman will be my new mother soon. I was so unhappy, that I had to run away. Father married this stranger, and once again and now we where in different country far away from each other. I wondered how long it would be before I'd see my father or other family again. I missed my father and my other sisters more and more every day. I also worried that they might be dead since we hadn't heard anything from them for over a year. I knew I was wallowing in self pity, but it was all getting to be too much for me. I just decided to think good thoughts and pray my other family was all right, and that they were hopefully living somewhere in Austria.

After I ran away from the kids, I took a walk to clear my head, and let my thoughts wander. I was thinking about my childhood and those carefree days, and I wasn't looking where I was going. Suddenly I realized I was almost to the village, and I didn't want to be there. What if I ran into some Russian soldiers? Just then I saw a big truck coming towards me full of Russian soldiers. I stopped in my tracks, turned and ran and I never ran so fast in my life. I stumbled over my own feet and fell flat on my face. Picking myself up, I ran, crying hysterically, not knowing or caring where I was going and not

Maria, Gypsy Princess

seeing anything. My knee hurt, the skin had broken, and it was bleeding, but I couldn't stop running.

I ran past the schoolhouse and headed out of town. I looked frantically for a place to hide, intent on getting away from the truck. I hadn't yet noticed it had turned off a while back. I ran deep into a wheat field, my heart pounding in my ears. I sat down and looked at my wounded knee. It was really sore. I pulled my dress over it and tried to wipe off some of the blood, but the blood had dried and wouldn't come off. I wet a corner of my dress with my spit, and wiped the dirt off the wound. There wasn't much else I could do now, so I sat in the middle of the field, pulled my legs up to my chest and rocked back and forth, humming a song my mother used to sing to me when I was little. I stayed that way a long, long time. Hours passed, and I was still sitting in the middle of the field, rocking back and forth.

In the meantime, Emma had come home from work and wanted to know where I was. Ida told her I went to play with some kids and one of them was Ermgard Kreuter, from upstairs. She was getting worried, because I had been gone a long time. So Ida went to ask Frau Kreuter if Ermgard knew where I was, but she said no, Mariechen left a long time ago. The kids told her I was crying, and Frau Kreuter didn't know where I went.

I must have stayed in that wheat field for hours because the sun was lowering in the West and I sat there all alone, my mind blank. I felt stiff all over. I had been in one position for so long I couldn't seem to move. I slowly got up and moved my legs to get the feeling back into them. My right knee was really sore, and I could hardly stand on it. I was scared to go home because I knew I would get it from Emma this time for sure. When I finally arrived home, I hesitated before entering. I was exhausted not looking forward to the licking I knew I would get. Emma was furious with me, getting red in the face, a shade of red I had never seen. I had never seen that look in her eyes either. I stood in front of her feeling small and weak. All I wanted was to hide under my bed covers and stay there forever. I kept standing there, waiting for something to happen, I didn't know what. Her hand came up so fast I didn't even see it, but I sure felt the sting when it connected with my cheek. I was so numb I didn't even flinch. I just stood there shriveled and beaten, not saying a word.

Ida came over and took me to my bunk bed and sat next to me. She asked where I had been. I could hardly hear her. My eyes were blurred and I didn't see a thing. She whispered into my ear, but I didn't respond. She finally eased me back on my pillow and lifted my legs up so I could lie flat. That's when she saw my knee, all swollen and inflamed. She must have motioned to Emma to come over because the next thing I felt on my sore knee was a cool, wet cloth. It felt good. I must've let out a deep sigh of relief, because I was being covered up and heard voices coming from far away as I dozed off. I don't know how long I was asleep, but when I slowly came back, I awoke to the wonderful aroma of food cooking. It seemed I was always waking to food cooking and a growling stomach.

I was facing the wall, and it took a few minutes to get my bearings. When I turned over, I saw a beautiful scene. Helmut and Hilde were playing choo, choo train on the floor not far from my bed. Emma, as always, was by the stove, and Ida was changing Inge. They were so engrossed in what they were doing they didn't pay any attention to me, and I enjoyed watching them for a few minutes and sending them my love. I thought, they are my family for the time being, and I was grateful for them. When she found out what made me run, Emma was very kind and loving and sorry she had hit me.

We'd been in that town for about six weeks when some of the families definitely decided to go back to Rumania; back to Alakap, to be precise, the village where most of us were born, and had left five years before. I, for one, didn't like the idea because it took us farther away from our father and sisters. Of course, I had nothing to say about it. Emma made all the decisions for us. A few days before we left I remember saying goodbye our other relatives and friends we been traveling with on the wagon train. It was a sad day for us all.

My aunt Sophia told me a few years later, after we came back to Wandersleben Germany that she should have held me back and kept me with them. But as she put it, "I was ill and not thinking straight and my strength at the time was low." I knew she had the same illness my mother had and didn't have much time to live. It was difficult for us to move on again, but after they made up their minds it didn't take us long to gather our belongings and move on. We were all so used to packing and loading our trunks on a big wagon or truck, it was second nature for us now. A big truck took us to the train station. Where we would board an old troop train, the boxcars were big, the kind used to haul livestock.

Chapter 13
Returning To Rumania 194

We were only a couple of months in East Germany and we were already leaving, like gypsies traveling to one place to another, looking for a new horizon, and a home to call our own. Traveling on a train and not by horse and wagon was a plus. About eight families were returning to Alakap. Some of our relatives came to the train and we said our tear full good-byes to them; they were smart enough not to go with us. They wished us well and God speed. I didn't cost us anything to be moved from one area to the next. Because in those days there were so many displaced people the government that was in charge at the time sent people to wherever they wanted to go, so not to over crowd one area.

It took a whole day and a lot of hands to load the boxcar with our stuff, but we were delayed and had to wait for our departure. The track we were to leave on was tied up with other traffic so we sat there for a whole week cooked our meals as before when we were on the wagon train. Our journey to Alakap took three months. We didn't arrive until November, 1945.

The trip itself was very hectic. Something always went wrong or someone got hurt. The children fought a lot because of the tight quarters, but that was life then. There wasn't any choice, our belongings were stacked on one side car and the rest of it was our living sleeping quarters. We slept on the floor of the car and used a chamber pot, also ate in our meals there when we were moving. The daily life was almost the same as when we were on the wagon train. When the train sat on a side track to let other traffic pass, we would sit around our campfire in the evening, cooking our meals and enjoying the lovely countryside; washing our clothes and taking care of the children who were in constant need and always asking for something we didn't have.

Again, we built open fire pits with stones and ate on makeshift tables and chairs. For drinking and cooking we fetched water from a river or someone's well. It was hard, but at least this time we didn't have to feed or water the horses.

Two families were assigned to one car evenly divided, ten to twelve persons in each. We shared with Jacob and Elisabeth Unrath who had nine children. One was Gottlieb, Emma's husband. Gottlieb and two of his brothers were in the army, and some of the Unrath's older children were married and weren't with us. There were six of them and six in our family. The car was crowded, but we made do.

We were a big, happy family, and everyone worked together for a common purpose and most times we all got along great. It was difficult at times to deal with so many people in a small area, but we were like brothers and sisters and closer than most real families. There were same disagreements and squabbles just like in all families.

We were held up a lot en route. Our train would be pushed to one side, and we sat there almost forgotten. We never knew how long we'd be stuck in one place. So the men and older boys, also some of the girls, would go to find odd jobs. They would bring us fresh fruit and vegetables and now and then fresh eggs and a chicken or two.

The first night, they put all the young children on top of the baggage to sleep. They were lined up in a row up there, and it seemed a good solution at first glance, until we heard crying and high pitched screams coming from the baggage area, and after the head count we found out Ida's daughter Inge was missing. We heard a muffled sound as if from far away. Ida was frantic. Inge was screaming and was wedged so deep between the wall of the car and the baggage we couldn't see her. We were baffled and didn't quite know where to look for her.

The train's movement must have bounced two-year-old Inge off the top, and she slid down the side of the car. She was lodged deep between the luggage and the wall. Our dilemma was how to extract her without harming her. It was a tricky situation to dislodge her without baggage falling and crushing her. Ida was screaming and trying to pull everything apart to get to Inge, but the men stopped her. They were scared she might pull out the wrong case and everything might fall on Inge. Emma and I held her back, She fought us with teeth and nails trying to get to her daughter.

I still can't figure how they got Inge out without her being hurt. But they did it, and we all thanked God for saving Inge - the second time in a few months. Whoever put those kids up there should've known not to put a two-year-old on the end of the row.

Day after day, the same chores had to be done; finding water and firewood to cook our meals. Washing clothes and bathing was a big problem for all. Every time we stopped for awhile, the men and some of the young people walked the streets again to find work. They were always lucky to bring back some fresh produce for all the families.

One day someone brought back a sack full of green apples, and I ate too many. That night we were all lying in our bedrolls, and a lot of snoring was going on, and I tried to shut them out and fall asleep, but to no avail. I lay there listening to all of them sawing logs. Then my stomach started to rumble and cramp. I had to get outside fast or I'd have an accident right there in my bedroll. I crawled and stumbled over the sleeping bodies on the way to the heavy door. My problem was, it was hard to open, and it took all my strength to pull back the heavy door. I was lucky to get out just in time, but as soon I was outside I could not hold on any longer. I crawled under the train, and it came shooting out of me, diarrhea from the green apples. I couldn't even get my panties' off before crap came out. So now my panties' were a mess and it was running down my legs.

The other problem, I had no toilet paper. How to clean myself up? So I crawled out from under the train. On the side were the fire pits, and looked I for anything I could use to clean myself. I spotted a bush and some grass a little way off so I headed for it, but that really didn't do the job very well. I knew I couldn't get back on the train smelling like a manure pile. I had to find another way. I browsed around and finally found a pail of water, and to my luck someone had left a towel lying near it. I took off my nightgown and washed myself all over, and also washed my pants and hung them over a bush.

Now I was afraid to go back to bed. What if I had to get out again? I waited for awhile to see if I had to go again, but I seemed to be all right. I grew tired so I finally went back into the car and lay down where I had a fitful sleep the rest of the night. I thank God I was okay the next day and it was only a one-time occurrence.

The trip was very long but also interesting. We traveled through three countries to reach Rumania, although we couldn't see much while we were moving. We passed through East Germany, the worst destruction was in Berlin, next through Hungary, and when we came to Budapest we were lucky to stop for a few days. Budapest, of course, is a very old, beautiful city, and we enjoyed staying there. There were interesting sights to see, but some parts were in ruins and the devastation was dreadful.

I thought we would never get to Alakap. First we went through Bucharest, then on to Constanta. From there we had to hire horses and wagons to get us to Alakap. It was slow going but we finally made it. Once again we had to find lodging and work. After both Emma and Ida found jobs, I had to take care of my three charges, Helmut, Hilde and Inge. A big job for a ten-year-old, but

Maria Reule Woelfl

I was their keeper for almost two years, from early morning until my sister came home at night from work.

Rumania seemed much different now than when we had lived there five years before. I didn't recognize most of it. Even our home seemed somehow different. It must have shrunk, because it looked so much smaller, not big and elegant as I remembered. When they say you can't go home again, it's true. Everything in the village had changed, and not for the better.

Our first home was with a Rumanian farmer woman who lived alone with her two children. She had a boy Helmut's age and a girl Inge's age. We rented a room off the stable, passing cows and chickens to get to our living quarters. The room had been used by farm workers in the past. There was a hearth on the stable side, and the room itself was very small. Just enough room for the five of us to sleep. Besides the beds, the only other furniture was a small, round table and two milking stools. Bunk beds on one side and a small bed against the other wall where Emma and Hilde slept. Helmut and I shared one bunk, and Ida and Inge shared the other. A little crowded but it was cozy. We had brought a big trunk with all our linens and some of our winter clothes. The trunk had to be stored just outside the room in the barn. There was a lock on the trunk, but if someone wanted to get into it, they could, and that is just what happened. The landlady stole some diaper cloth from the trunk. She was smart enough to dye it but because of the pattern in the fabric we could tell it belonged to us, but without proof, there was nothing to be done.

After Ida and Emma found work, I looked after the kids. We would wander through the village, all three kids on a string. I felt they were mien now because I'd been their mother and father for the last two years. The four of us were really something to see. You might have seen some film in your life where a young girl schleps her younger brothers and sisters around. Well, that was me. I put Inge on my hip and wrapped a long cord around my middle and tied Hilde and Helmut on it. I held Hilde's hand and Helmut tagged along behind. That's how we trekked through the village.

We'd visit some of the other families, and most of the time we'd go to Helmut's and Hilde's grandparents. That was great for me because there were always other kids to play with. That gave me a little free time for myself. So I'd go outside, and to amuse myself I'd make a doll out of matches. I took a small box of matches and pretended the part you light was the head of the doll. Then I'd take another match and tie it crossways, then wrap it in a tiny cloth and use the box for its bed. I was content playing with that doll and matchbox for an hour, that's if I had some free time. I loved it. As long as I was left alone, I was happy. In those days we were happy with very little.

We had to make our own fun. We only got things that didn't cost money. Everything was homemade and we didn't need or want anything else.

Emma was my sore point, because any time something went wrong I would get it. One day I took the kids for a long walk through the village to visit a few relatives. Alas that day I came home and found the sack of cornmeal we kept in the corner next to the big trunk was scattered all over the stable. That morning the sack was almost full, but when I returned it was only one quarter left.

I knew I would get blamed for not being home and watching our belongings. When Emma came home and found out, she was livid. We knew right away where the extra cornmeal went. It was stolen by our landlady. But, of course, we couldn't prove it, so for now we could do anything about it. Cornmeal was dear so my sisters had to work extra hours to make up for the loss.

Emma asked the landlady what happened to the cornmeal, and she told Emma the cow got lose and wandered over and ate most of it before she could stop her. We knew it was a lie, but couldn't prove it so there was nothing to do but lock up everything in our room, what we should have done in the first place. Live and learn, as the saying goes.

The days ran into each other, and the chores were always the same. Sundays were a little different because Emma and Ida had the day off. Then they took care of their kids, and I had some time for myself. We also had a great Sunday dinner that Emma cooked. Roast chicken or pork was usually Sunday fare. Side dishes were mostly strudel and red cabbage or green beans and a flan or streusel Kuchen for dessert. It was enjoyed by all, and that day we spent time with each other and talked about how our week went and what we did.

In the evenings the kids and I went to the top bunk and cuddled, and I told them fairy tales, the same stories my father used to tell when I was their age. They, in turn would run their fingers over my arms and legs and comb my hair. It felt so good that I almost fell asleep, but they always woke me up with, "Mariechen, one more, please." That's what I always said when I was little and father told me stories.

"One more, Papa," I would say.

Inge was sickly like her mother. There was always something wrong with her. The poor thing was so constipated she screamed and screamed when she was unable to have a bowel movement. It was so bad that her hemorrhoids came all the way out and were all red, and you could see the hard as a rock stool trying to push out, but it wouldn't come out. Both Ida and Emma were worried that she would hurt herself pushing so hard. They sent me to Emma's in-laws to ask what to do, and her mother-in-law made up a remedy from some herbs and gave me some special salve to put on her bottom to take away the inflammation. Emma boiled water, put the herbs in it and let it steep awhile, and after it cooled she put it in a bottle and gave it to Inge to drink. Inge quieted down after she drank the brew and dozed off.

It took about four hours to work and it still hurt her a lot, but after the real hard stuff came out the rest was easier and she felt better. It was short lived because a couple of weeks later Inge got sores all over her head. It was ringworm and we had to cut off all her beautiful curly blond hair, and again she was in pain. I also got sores, but mine were all over my legs. It was severe and hard to heal. Emma put some sulfur in a bowl and lit it, and Inge and I sat under a blanket and the smoke from the sulfur did the job, but it took quire awhile to heal the sores. My biggest problem was winter. Now I wore long knit stockings, and every time I pulled them off the sores would reopen and hurt and bleed, so they took longer to heal.

When Emma and Ida's day work was done, they had to go out and find new jobs. Both found work on a big farm with lots of cattle and horses. We were happy to get away from the woman who kept stealing from us.

Again we had a room off the stable but much bigger and nicer. Ida and Inge had their own room in the main house. Ida was to work in the household, help with cooking and making the beds, while Emma worked in the fields. I was glad it worked out that way because Ida was ill and she looked more drawn every day. She shouldn't work so hard, and with her illness being out in the sun was bad for her. She was getting worse. She should have been in a sanitarium instead of working on a farm.

Ida was such a brave soul. I never heard her complain about anything, and she was quiet and reserved. She took care of her daughter and kept to herself. In all the years I knew her she never once scolded me. I always thought the saying, "the good die young" was wrong, but it applied to my sister, Ida. She had such a big heart and loving ways. She reminded me of our mother. Emma wasn't kind and loving too; but she just had to be the strong one of the family.

Even I had to help in the kitchen sometimes because it was a big household with a lot of people to be fed. We all worked from early morning into the night before we could rest; it was a hard life for all of us.

Our room had two beds and a small table with a couple of chairs. I had a bed made of straw on the floor. It was comfortable and I didn't mind it at all. A few days after we arrived, there was a commotion outside. I was in the small entry hall of our room, and being nosy I took a chair and looked out the high window to see what was going on. I was astounded by what I saw. They were leading two horses on a rope, and the bigger of the two was circling the mare and sniffing around her. The female stood very still while the stud whinnied and snorted. He was hard to handle. He kept circling, sniffing her behind. She then lifted her tail while he stood very close, and as I stood there, his member came out. I had never seen anything so big.

It was big and black and as long and thick as a man's arm. I shouldn't have watched, but I could not tear myself away. The stallion lifted his front legs and put them on top of the mare, then put his member inside her, and she still didn't move. He did his job and jumped off, and he was a little giddy. The men had a red liquid in a pail that they poured on the steed's member. Then they took him back to his stall. The show was over, but it was exciting while it lasted. I climbed down quickly. I didn't dare tell what I had seen because I would have been punished. I had seen two dogs together but never something like this.

I still took care of the kids and didn't go to school all the while we were in Rumania. Now that the harvest was in, there wasn't enough work for both Emma and Ida, so Emma had to go look for work elsewhere and also find us new lodgings. A few weeks later Ida lost her job too, so they both started to work as day laborers and took jobs wherever anyone needed something done. It was a hard winter, and we now lived in a regular house with a Bulgarian family. They had just one big room and a smaller one for cooking their meals, while we had two nice sized rooms. One had a stove, a table and chairs and even a dresser. There were two beds in the back where Ida and I slept, and Emma and her kids slept in the bigger room with a large bed where the stove was.

My job was to find something to heat the rooms with and fuel for cooking. It was winter now and slim pickings when it came to fire materials. The other family had some cows and chickens, so they sold us milk and eggs. After they cleaned the stall, the straw and manure were stacked in a big pile in the yard, and that's what we used for heating and cooking. When the straw froze it was almost impossible to pull apart, but that was one of my many jobs, pulling the straw apart, then bringing it in to make a fire in the stove each morning. I also went out and picked up whatever I could find in the way of fuel, corncobs and cow droppings made a better fire and lasted longer than straw. The straw had to be fed into the stove every few minutes or you couldn't cook anything, because it burned down too fast. Helmut and I would go and find cow droppings and put them in a place to dry to be used for fuel later.

Five people lived in the other room, a man and his two girls and two boys. They didn't have a mother. One of the girls was my age. Her brother, Serge, was a couple years older and the twins were eight years old. Their place was very dark and dreary and they did everything in it; they lived slept and ate there. I don't think they ever cleaned it. The room smelled awful and was

Maria Reule Woelfl

really smoky inside. I was sure they all had lice too. I tried to stay away from them as much as possible because I was afraid of getting lice again. Once was enough!

They had a sled, and we all took turns going down the hill in front of the house. When it came my turn, I lay on the sled and asked Serge to push me. He did, and ran beside me for awhile, but then he jumped on top of me and lay there all the way down the hill. I tried to push him off, but he was too strong for me, and when we got to the bottom I was very angry and slapped him. I didn't like the idea of him being on top of me. What if I caught something from him? Or what if I got pregnant? I had no idea where babies came from yet. I still believed the stork brought them to families who wanted them. You might think that watching the horses and all the other animals having their young I wouldn't be so naïve, but it didn't occur to me that people did the same thing animals did. That would be too icky!

So the winter went on and time slowed, and I had a lot of work to do. Start the fire in the morning, keep it going, put water on to cook cornmeal mush and heat the milk to pour on top of it. That was our breakfast most mornings. Then take care of the kids all day. It was really cold when I got out of bed and not easy to keep the fire lit, feeding the flames with straw. Cooking that way was almost impossible.

In the spring of 1946 we found out that our oldest sister, Anna, and her four children where living in Constanta . Her husband was in the German army too, and she left Poland the same time we left Yugoslavia . She came to Rumania right away because her husband, Johan, told her he would meet her in Rumania after the war was over. That's why she took her three boys and her daughter, Maria, to Constanta , where they had lived before leaving Rumania in 1940. Maria was named after me and was only two years younger. I went to visit Anna in Constanta and stayed with her for a week. It was great being together again. I hadn't seen her since we left Rumania and hadn't met her boys yet.

Anna hadn't changed much. She was always very slim with a strong personality. She liked to bargain for everything and never paid full price. Even when she went to stores and there was a price tag on something, she would still ask how much, then tell the person it was too much money and leave the store. She would return the next day and ask how much again. She did that until she wore that person out then got the best price. Then she walked out of the store smiling. As I said, Anna was foxy, and stayed that way all of her life.

Later, when the time came for us to leave Rumania and take the last train to freedom, Anna chose to stay behind and wait for her husband to return from the war. It didn't matter that she hadn't heard from him in years. She knew in her heart if he was still alive he would meet her just where he said he would. You couldn't budge her from her spot and the life she had made for her family there. She would do any job, even steal to feed her children. I am sure she did a lot of that in the years she lived there. Anna's husband did come back and the family stayed in Rumania.

When we left from Constanta on that last train for freedom, Anna and the kids were there to bid us farewell. A lot of tears were shed. We knew it would be a long time before Emma would write a letter. I don't think she has ever written one in her life. I know it was because of lack of schooling. She went only to Rumanian school when we first lived there. I am sure it was because she had to go to work when she was very young.

Chapter 14
Return from Rumania

We took the last train out before the border closed. It would be years before they opened it again. The reason we didn't see Anna and her family for years was that Rumania fell behind the Iron Curtain, the same as East Germany did. Anna and her children remained behind and lived in the city of Constanta all those years. Rumania was Communistic under Russian influence when we left there. Therefore, they weren't able to leave until the curtain came up and the border opened in the 1980s, the same as East Germany.

The journey back to Wandersleben East Germany was much easier than the trip to Rumania two years earlier. These were lean years and it was especially bad living in the East Zone. The Russians sent all the produce that hard working Germans so painfully scratched out of the earth to Mother Russia; while the people in East Germans worked for slave wages, and the little money they did receive didn't help much because there was hardly anything in the stores to buy. The shelves were almost bare.

Our relatives who stayed there were fortunate to live in a small village where one could have a vegetable garden and raise a few chickens and even pigs. Of course, the people weren't allowed to keep all of it, but it was still better than living in a big city. It took a lot of work and energy to make ends meet from 1945 to the 1980s.

I don't remember much about the return train trip from Rumania, but we were all elated when we finally arrived in Wandersleben. I was hoping now that we were back in a civilized country and surrounded by family and friends, everything would fall into place and I would be reunited with my father and other sisters.

Of course, it didn't turn out that way. I had forgotten we were dealing with the Russians and not the Germans. The Russians were a cruel and greedy people and enjoyed their power and booty from the spoils of war. I

Maria, Gypsy Princess

was thankful our family was still alive and our father and sisters were living in lower Austria in the state of Kärnten, in a small village of Graffendorf. Knowing that made me happy, but it didn't help much because I still wasn't able to go to be with them. Being behind the iron curtain had many draw backs, and I had no idea how I would get to Austria to be reunited with my family. My first aim was to get to West Germany. I had to be happy with one step at a time and hope it would take me back to where I belonged.

A new adventure started for Emma, Helmut, Hilde and me. Aunt Sophia and Uncle William Schelske took us in when we arrived in Wandersleben. They didn't have enough room for Ida and Inge so they went to live with our Uncle Johannes Reule and his family. I really missed them. We had become a close knit family while in Rumania. For two years I was the children's mother while Ida and Emma worked to put food on the table.

I was eleven years old now and had to go to school with the third graders who were all eight or nine year olds, children compared to me. It was difficult making friends because of the age difference, and not having proper clothes to wear didn't help the matter either. I remember an incident when my Aunt Lidia made me a dress out of flannel material. It looked like a nightgown, but I had to wear it because it was a gift and I had outgrown most everything I owned. My cousin Edmund Reule was the bad seed in this tale. He was teasing me at recess in the schoolyard. My only new friend was Christa, she and I were playing touch ball, and the boys were being a nuisance. They were trying to take the ball from us, and my cousin Edmund finally did. I went after him, grabbed the ball out of his hands and ran with it. That made him angry because he couldn't run as fast as I could. So he stopped chasing me and started chanting, "Maria is wearing a nightgown, Maria is wearing a nightgown." The other boys took up the chant and circled me, chanting and laughing. At first, I ran after Edmund saying, "Wait till I get you!"

But when they didn't let up, my feelings were hurt and I started to cry uncontrollable sobs. Christa came and tried to comfort me, but I was out of control. When the bell rang for us to go back into the classroom I was still crying. I sat in my chair put my head on my desk and my body shook all over with sobs.

When the teacher came in she was surprised it was so quiet. She looked around and that's when she heard my sobs. I was hiccupping now, my eyes all red and swollen. She came over to me and asked what the matter was. I couldn't get the words out, so the girl sitting next to me told her what had happened. The teacher called Edmund over and told him he had to apologize to me. He just stood there saying nothing. The teacher Frau Nobel pulled his ear and told him again to say he was sorry. She finally got a small sorry out of him. Then she made him stand in the corner, and in a loud voice told him,

Maria Reule Woelfl

"I'll deal with you later. She then told us, to get your books out and told Olga to start reading where we left off earlier.

Olga's voice shook and she shuddered while reading. The teacher finally called on someone else to read and afterward we went on to arithmetic. By then I had settled down enough to concentrate, so I put my hand up because numbers were my favorite subject. I gave the teacher the correct answer, and she was pleased that I had stopped crying. So we went on with our lessons the rest of the day.

School let out and on the way home a lot of the kids came over and sympathized with me. My friend Christa and I walked together until she had to turn off to her for home. We promised to meet at the same place the next day so we could walk to school together. When I arrived home, my Aunt Sophia gave me a snack of an apple and a glass of milk. She told me I had to take care of Hilde and Helmut until Emma came in from the field. So my freedom was short lived.

It was all right. I was used to it since I had been doing it for years now. I was really more worried about Ida and Inge than about myself. We hadn't heard from them for awhile, and I knew Ida was very ill and probably didn't have much more time to live.

Day in and day out everything was the same and time went very slowly. School work, a little free time once in awhile, and that felt good. On my free time I loved to just be by myself or visit and play with my friends. My cousin Rosa and I spent a lot of time gossiping together.

The episode with my cousin Edmund was forgotten and I forgave him. His mother punished him. After all, Aunt Lidia was the one who made the dress for me.

The little house we lived in was over crowded with the four of us and the Schelske's family, which made eight. Sometimes we felt packed in like sardines. Emma had her own bedroom, and the kids slept with her. I slept in a narrow bed in the entry hall to Emma's room.

I felt I didn't belong anywhere or to anyone, like an abandoned and very lonely child. Most of my young life I had been shuffled around from one country to another.

Emma must have felt the same loneliness. After all, she hadn't seen or heard from her husband in years. None of us knew where he was, if he was still alive or if he would ever come back from the war.

As we found out later Emma's husband Gottlieb was in a Russian prison. He came back from Russia in 1949, a long time to spend in such a hell hole. He lost sixty pounds while there.

School got better because I made more friends. I enjoyed learning. I had missed a lot in the last two years, but my teacher was a gem and that's always a plus.

It was the first of May, and we all celebrated May Day with a pole dance in the park. It was a lot of fun seeing the girls' colorful dirndls flaring out, and the boys with their Lederhosen were fetching. They danced around the May pole while the colorful ribbons wrapped themselves around it. It was wonderful to watch. There was always a lot of good food and drink at such occasions and it was a great day. Spring dragged on, but the summer as always seemed to go too fast. All of us enjoyed the freedom because of no school for awhile.

September came and there was a problem with the potato crop. Thousands of little bugs were chomping away on the potato leaves. They had to be dealt with right away or the whole crop would be lost. So all the classes were recruited, and we children went out every afternoon after school and picked the little buggers off the leaves.

They would pick us up at school, load us on wagons and drive us out to the potato fields. We would pick the bugs off the leaves and put them into pails. They were then burned in a furnace, "broiled bugs" we called them. We worked for weeks until they were under control. We kids saved the crop that year!

I remember we'd get care packages from the U.S. and would all flock around when they arrived. This particular day I was really happy because in one package was a dress that fit me like a dress should and also looked like one and not a nightgown. I had never seen such a beautiful dress. It was dark blue with short sleeves and twenty or thirty tiny buttons running down the front, and the buttons were just there for show.

It was just a little too long for me, but easy to shorten. I was so proud of that dress. I wore it to school the next day to show it off. There were a lot of other things in those packages, shoes none of us could wear because they were too narrow and our wide feet didn't fit into them. It was easy to make me happy in those times, especially getting something for my very own. Happiness was also when my sister gave me an hour or two of freedom to do what ever I wanted.

Most of these times I spent alone day dreaming, or my cousin Rosa and I would do something together. Rosa was the daughter of Aunt Lidia by her first marriage. She married Uncle Daniel after his first wife and his oldest daughter Sophia died of tuberculosis. My cousin Erika was the daughter from Uncle Daniel's first marriage. Edmund was the child of their union. So the family was my child, your child and our child. Edmund was the one who was so mean to me in the schoolyard. That brat.

Rosa and I would go into the garden and sit under a big apple tree and just talk. She was three years older and already had her period and told me all about it. But what she told me was puzzling. "Why?" I would ask, "Do girls have periods and boys don't?"

"I don't know," She said.

She told me when she first discovered blood in her underpants she was really scared because she had no idea what was happening to her. She went to her older stepsister Erika and asked about it, and Erika sent her to her mother to explain it.

"Well, did she explain?" I asked.

"Not really. She told me that it happens to all girls when they get to a certain age. Then she told me, "From now on I have to be careful and stay away from boys.""

"What does that mean," I asked, "away from boys?"

She shook her head. "I don't know. I guess no kissing or holding hands. Your guess is as good as mine."

About a week later it was just another day of freedom, and this time I was asked to stay for supper with the Reule's. After dinner I helped with the dishes and Rosa walked me part way home. We said our good nights and I walked the rest of the way alone.

It was a real dark night without stars or moon visible, and I couldn't see where I was going. While walking it felt like I was climbing a hill, and suddenly I fell into nothingness and landed on top of a wheelbarrow on the other side of the pile of manure I had climbed up. When I fell on the metal wheelbarrow I hurt my shin and it was bleeding and painful.

I was howling when I came into the house. Everyone was alarmed and wanted to know what was wrong with me. I showed them my shin, and they couldn't figure out how I had fallen onto the wheelbarrow in the first place. It was my bad luck that the wheelbarrow was standing on that side. When I fell on it, it took a big gash out of my shin. When I got up, I could hardly walk. My Aunt Sophia saw me first, jumped up, asked me what happened and I told her.

Emma went and brought a washbasin with warm water and a washcloth, cleaned the wound and put some salve on it. That made it feel much better, and my tears dried up. I still have the scar. Just another day in the life of Maria.

One day we received a telegram, and I was elated, jumping up and down. I could hardly wait for someone to open it. When Emma finally opened it and read it, it seemed the words that came out of her mouth could not be true. I didn't want to believe them. It was such a great shock to hear our sister Ida had died. All the joy drained out of me and I started to cry. Our wonderful sister Ida had died a few hours before. "I am sorry, Maria," said Emma, "but you shouldn't feel so happy until you find out the message in a telegram." I couldn't stop crying. I would never see Ida again, and I wasn't able to say goodbye to her and what about Inge? We couldn't even go to the funeral because she lived to far away, in the town of Fernstead and she was to be buried there. I still don't know why we didn't go to the funeral. It was such a sad time. We should have made an effort to go and be with Inge. It wasn't right to leave her alone with strangers without a mother or father.

Inge at four

Poor Inge was all alone now. The letter we had received from Ida a month before sounded so sad and lonely. She and Inge shouldn't have been left with Aunt Christine. She was not a nice lady. If you read between the lines in Ida's letter you could tell they didn't have an easy life with Uncle Johannes and Aunt Christine.

Now she was gone and little Inge was an orphan. None of us knew where her father, Joseph was, or even if he was still alive. I found out years later that Joseph had survived the war and instead of looking for his family he went back to his home town in the Steirmark. He didn't know if Ida and Inge were alive or dead but he married a home town girl and they had a daughter together. My niece Inge told me about this in 1987 when I visited her and her family in Bad Herzfeld. At that time she was thinking of going to visit her half-sister. But I don't think she ever did, unless she did it in the last two years?

I was proud of my father because when he found out Ida had died he started papers right away to have Inge brought to Austria to live with our family. I had no idea he had done that until later, and it was so like him. At

Maria Reule Woelfl

the same time he found a way to get me back to West Germany and to Austria where they lived now.

'Life went on as usual, school, work and a little fun now and then. I was so used to the routine I took it for granted. My friend Christa and I spent a lot of time together while I was waiting for my father to bring me home. It didn't matter where this home was. I felt wherever my father was, that was home to me. It took five more months to finally be reunited with my father and family.

My Aunt Lidia's, Brother Christian Blumhagen came to visit his sister in Wandersleben. He lived in Ludwigsburg, West Germany and he was to take me over the boarder. I had no idea my father had written to all his brothers and sisters to find someone who was going to East Germany. My cousin Christian came for a visit in the winter of '47 and stayed with his sister for a week. He told me my father had written him to bring me to the West. I wondered how he would accomplish that feat, but when the time came for him to leave he told me to get ready. I was to take very little with me, only what I could easily carry. I had a small case and a rucksack and he didn't have much more than I. The farewell was very difficult for me. After all, I had been with Emma and the children for over four years now, and we were almost connected by the hip. I would miss them but I was also excited to be going on another adventure, this time taking me home to my father. I would also miss my aunts uncles and cousins but I was still happy to be going home.

It was a real adventure for both Christian and me to walk across the mountain from the East to the West. Christian and I left on a train from Erfurt, a city fifty kilometers from Wandersleben. Someone borrowed a car to take us there, and we bought two tickets at the station and stayed on the train until we came to the town of Achenbach. Every time the train stopped at a station, German police came on to stamp our tickets and look at Christian's passport and stamp it too. The first time the East German patrol came through the train, I was scared they would take me off and send me back to Wandersleben. But everything went smoothly until we had to leave the train and go by foot. Achenbach was the last station in East Germany. Christian and I then went looking for a guide to take us over the mountains into West Germany.

Christian

It seemed as if we walked for hours, looking for the right person to show us the way. We finally found someone to guide us. He took us by truck as far as we could go and then we had to go on by foot. We went up a hill through a mountain pass where the snow was up to my arm pits. Christian had to give the man fifty West Marks and some of the food we had brought with us for payment. He walked with us up this steep hill for a quarter of a mile up and then turned back. He told us to go straight up and over the top and the other side would be West Germany.

Well, it was easier said than done. The snow was getting deeper the farther up we went, and more difficult to walk. The snow was so deep in some areas I got stuck and couldn't move forward. Christian gave me his suitcase to carry and put his hands on my back and pushed me up the mountain. We both were huffing and puffing by the time we reached the top. That's when we saw a train coming in the distance and we were elated to see the train station below us. We stopped to rest a few minutes before we went on. When we started again, hurrying down the other side, I fell and tumbled a long way down the mountain, Christian chasing after, trying to catch me. I was lucky to land in a ravine and stop from rolling all the way down onto the train tracks.

I thanked God for watching over me and letting me halt in a ravine and not on the tracks. Christian knelt next to me with a worried look and asked, "Are you alright?" I just nodded because the wind had been knocked out of me and for a minute I couldn't speak. He lifted me up and checked me over to see if I had broken anything, but I seemed to be okay.

"Can you move?" he asked. I tried my legs. They were a little wobbly but otherwise fine. "Okay, let's cross over to the "WEST."

I was sure glad I was wearing ski pants and boots because I was soaking wet, but thank God I didn't feel cold. The excitement must have kept me warm.

When we finally arrived at the station, we were still in East Germany and the train was just pulling in. Only a few people were on the train, they all had to get off to be searched. The East German police had to make sure no one without papers slipped through their fingers. After all the people got back on the train, they came to us. What if they sent me back? I didn't have any papers or passport to cross the border.

The police control looked at Christian's passport and wanted to know why his passport wasn't stamped from the last station where it stopped. There was nothing else to do but tell them the truth. Two officers took us aside, and Christian explained what we did and told them the whole story. After he finished they asked me how old I was and what year I was born. I told them I was born in 1935 and I would be 12 years old March, 8. They both looked at me to see if I was lying, but to my relief they believed me. So they told us it was okay for me to cross to the West because I was under 12 years of age. I let out a sigh when I heard the good news. My relief must have shown because the policemen smiled at me.

They told Christian he had to pay a fine of fifty Marks again. One of them said the money was because we tried to take advantage of the East German people and it had to be West Marks. I looked at Christian, and I was worried because I didn't know if he had another fifty Marks to give them, after paying the guide. They also wanted some of our food. We didn't have too much left, but were so happy they let us go we gladly gave them some worst and bread. We had only enough for two small meals for ourselves, and it had to last us until we got where we were going; the last leg of our trip was uneventful and I, for one, was glad. I'd had enough excitement to last a lifetime.

When we finally settled into the train, I was still apprehensive and could not sit still. But as soon the train started to move I let out another sigh and relaxed. I hadn't realized I'd been holding my breath so long. I sat by the window, so tired I leaned into the corner I fell fast asleep.

When I awoke the compartment was almost full of people. I sat up and looked around, confused. I must have looked a sight, disheveled and dirty, because people were staring at me, wrinkling their noses as if smelling something foul. I was sure it was me they smelled. I hadn't looked in a mirror since early that morning. When I glanced down at myself, I saw my clothes were caked with mud and my hair was hanging in tangles down my shoulders. No wonder they all looked at me with disdain.

Maria, Gypsy Princess

These good people must have thought; "WHAT A DIRTY GYPSY!"

I asked Christian where the bathroom was. I at least could go see what I looked like and maybe do some repair to make myself more presentable. Christian stood, guided me past the legs of the people and showed me where to go.

I did look a sight, like death warmed over. My face was drawn and smeared with dirt and my hair a tangled mess. I did all I could, but it was a losing battle. I washed my face and hands then ran my fingers through my hair. That had to do for now.

When I came back to the compartment the overall feeling seemed much friendlier. At first I couldn't figure out why their attitude had changed towards for the better. It finally dawned on me that Christian must have told them of our ordeal. Everyone in the compartment smiled at me now, some even squeezed my hand. I sat back down and told Christian I was hungry, and that made everyone smile even more. The lady next to me stood, pulled a basket down from the luggage rack and started taking food out of it. She cut a slice of bread, put butter and worst on it and offered it to me. I looked at Christian with hungry eyes.

"Its okay, Maria he said, go ahead and take it."

I thanked the lady and hungrily bit into the bread and sausages. It really tasted good and I was grateful for being there. Other people took down baskets and offered Christian food too and we all ate happily, chatting about our trip. For dessert someone gave me some fruit and a piece of Kuchen. Everything was delicious, and now I was really tired. The long climb had taken more out of me than I thought. My clothes were wet and uncomfortable which didn't help. The lady next to me, Frau Kessler, said, "Why don't you sleep awhile," and moved to the other side so I could stretch out. She noticed my boots were soaked through, so she helped me take them off and even gave me some dry socks. She folded my coat under my head, put a big shawl over me, and I was asleep in minutes.

This time I had wonderful dreams. I dreamed my mother was rocking me in her arms singing to me, and Father was watching us and smiling.

Chapter 15

When I awoke we were pulling into a West German station. Germany had changed drastically in the last few years, and there was a huge difference between East and West. It was winter, of course, and cold and dreary, but the towns and surrounding areas were so much nicer here. The buildings were clean and freshly painted and the streets had no potholes. Everything looked wonderful. I had spent so many years in poverty and dirt; I finally felt I had come home. The people were smiling and friendly. It was unbelievable that both sides were the same country and they were all Germans, that a few miles could make such a difference between peoples' looks and attitudes.

It took a couple of days to reach our destination. Christian delivered me to my Aunt Bertha and Uncle Heinrich Sommer's home, and Christian went back home to Ludwigsburg were he lived.

Aunt Bertha was my father's youngest sister, and I was to stay with them for awhile. I hadn't seen them since 1941 when we left Geras, Austria. They lived near Karlsruhe in the town of Jockgrim. They had three boys. Aunt Bertha was only two years older then my oldest sister, Anna, and I didn't know her well. In the past she had always been nice and friendly but a little standoffish. I was greeted with open arms and they made me welcome in their home. My nephews were lively young boys. Herbert was six, Hilbert was four, and baby Igor a year old. I share a bed with the two boys. That didn't bother me because I was used to sharing beds. I kept the boys interested telling them fairy tales, the same ones my father told us when I was little. Again I was entertaining the younger generation with the same stories.

There wasn't any school in the village so I didn't go to school right away. I helped Aunt Bertha with the household chores and took care of the kids sometimes. I still had a lot of free time to explore the village and its people. They were really nice and treated me kindly. I had to make new friends again and that wasn't easy, but I didn't mind. The last few years I had a lot of practice making new friends.

The plan was I would stay with them for a month then go stay with my Aunt Else Kutz in Sersheim for awhile. I was to stay with them until my sister Gottliebe came to take me to the Austrian border by train. Then the Red Cross would deliver me to Kärnten where my father lived now.

My father had planned it all out. I was to come home as soon as possible, but alas sometimes plans fall through and I had to be patient a little longer. Idleness didn't agree with me, so I was glad to go back to school and loved it. I walked five kilometers to school every day, to and fro and I made new friends too and it was great.

One rainy Saturday afternoon we were all stuck in the house, so I invited some of my new found friends to play. My aunt and uncle went to a party that afternoon and took the younger boys but left me in charge of Herbert. She put down some guidelines, and went on and on with her dos and don'ts. I listened, nodding and saying, "Ja, ja ich verstehe, aufwiedersehn." (I understand, good bye for now).

After they left, a few more kids came by to play. One was our tutor, Erik Blaum. He was much older than the rest of us, seventeen or eighteen and very handsome. I had a crush on him. While we were playing hide and seek, I hid in one of the upstairs bedrooms under the bed. I was there quite awhile, and no one came to find me. I was about to go see where everyone was when I heard someone coming, so I scooted back under the bed and kept quiet. The door opened and squeaked a little, and I could tell it wasn't one of the little kids. At first I thought my uncle had come back to get something, and I was very still and held my breath. I heard the closet door open and someone moving hangers and boxes around in there. I wasn't sure who it was, but he or she sat on the bed and started bouncing up and down, laughing. It sounded like Erik, our young student teacher. Just as I suspected it was him, he started too bounce and chant, "Come out, come out, wherever you are." I didn't know what to do. I was getting cramps and the bouncing hit my head. Finally I told him to stop, it was hurting me. He knelt and pulled me out.

"Well," he said, "you sure found a good hiding place. It took me a long time to find you. I stood up and he laughed and reached for me. I tried to get away and stumbled, grabbing onto the bedspread not to fall. He caught me or I would've hit my head on the corner of a dresser.

"Boy, that was close," he said as he pulled me onto the bed and sat next to me. "Are you alright?"

I nodded, flustered because his arms were around me made me feel funny and warm all over. I had never felt anything like that before. I shyly turned and looked at him. He was gorgeous! His arms felt so good, I didn't want to move away from him. But just then one of the other kids ran in and shouted, "Here they are. I found them. I found them. I get the prize, I get the prize!"

The great moment was gone. Eric squeezed my shoulders once more, bent and moved his lips ever so slightly over my cheek. Then he got up. I must have blushed because this warm feeling came over me. It felt good. I was sorry he got up. That was my first encounter with the feeling of love, or close to it.

I was glad when the party broke up because I wanted to go somewhere and dream about the time with Erik. I could still feel his arm around me and I felt special and grown up. My whole body was tingling. After that day every time I saw Erik, I flushed all over, lowered my eyes when he looked at me, and turned away so he couldn't see me bushing. It was a great feeling and I wallowed in it for quite awhile. I thought I was in love with my teacher, but alas it was just a crush and a daydream. After all, he was too old for me.

As the days passed I got interested in other things. My feelings for him slowly ebbed, but I stored the memories in a secret corner of my heart, safely tucked away to dream on.

I had been there four weeks now and just when I was getting used to their way of life; Uncle Emil Kutz came to pick me up to go stay with them for awhile. They lived in Sersheim not far from Stuttgart. I enjoyed the trip because he had borrowed a car, and it was like being on an outing.

My grandmother and grandfather Reule lived with them and it was great seeing them again. Grandma and grandpa had a little apartment across the street from Aunt Else and Uncle Emil. After we arrived and said our hellos, I went to visit with my grandmother. She had stomach cancer and had been bedridden for quite awhile now. She looked tired and could hardly talk. She recognized me, though, and that pleased me. We had a nice visit and conversation. I remember her as a kind and loving soul, always good to all her grandchildren with kind words for us and always offering us something she had just baked, warm out of the oven.

I was six years old the last time we saw each other when we lived in Austria it the Cloister. She wanted me to tell my father how she missed him, especially how he used to help her in the kitchen when he was a boy. That made us both giggle because we knew how much my father hated kitchen work.

Once again I had to fit in and adapt to a new family. Of course, I'd had plenty of practice adapting and fitting in to all kinds of places. I was grateful to my extended family for being so good to me. They all took me in and treated me as if I was one of their own children. I stayed with the Kutz family a few weeks, and while I was there my Grandmother died. Another death in my family. My sister Ida had just died a few weeks before. So much sadness and loss in my life. I had enough. PLEASE NO MORE, GOD.

Maria, Gypsy Princess

The funeral was a small affair, just family and a few friends to bid her a fond farewell and pay their last respects to a wonderful woman. I got to see other relatives I hadn't seen since we left Austria. Sad reunion, but great spending time with them, reminiscing about the old days. The only thing I didn't like about the funeral was the open casket, having to gaze at a dead person gives me nightmares.

Grandpa Reule was now a shrunken man. He lived to be eighty-eight years old and died in 1958 in Sersheim. When I was small I thought of him as a fierce force. All of us young cousins were scared of him. Sometimes we were invited to dinner at Grandma and Grandpa's house. Of course, they couldn't invite the whole family at the same time. because there were too many. Two or three of the Reule children and their families would be invited for Sunday dinner at their home. There was always a children's table in the kitchen, far from the adults. Sometimes older boys and girls could sit with the grown ups, but if any talked without being asked, grandpa would look at them sternly and say, "Don't you have something in front of you to stuff in your mouth?"

Can you imagine what it was like when all the Reule clan went there for dinner? When we were all there the tables were setup out in the yard for a party of forty or fifty people. Everyone brought something to eat. It was always fun, the wine flowed freely and the older grandchildren would get a small glass watered down wine with their dinner.

In the summer of 1948 Gottliebe came to take me to the Austrian border. We went by train to Salzburg. She had written a letter to the Red Cross in Salzburg and a Red Cross nurse was to come to the station to pick me up. The Red Cross nurses were instrumental in reuniting me with my father.

Gottliebe and I arrived at dusk, and she went and telephone and notify the Red Cross office that we were at the train station on the German side. We waited outside on a bench for about a half-hour before a Red Cross vehicle stopped in front of us. A lovely young lady stepped out. "Gutten Abent," she said, "Sind Sie Frau Horling, und ist dieses Madchen, Freulein Reule?"

Gottliebe said, "Yes I am Frau Horling, and this is my sister Maria Reule. She's the one traveling with you to Kärnten, Friesach. Our father Gottlieb Reule will pick her up there."

"I know," she said, "my name is Freulein Strauss, and I'll be in charge of Maria's travels. She'll stay at our headquarters tonight and be in Friesach Wednesday at 5:00 in the evening."

"Will someone travel with her?" Gottliebe asked.

"No, we think Maria is old enough to travel by herself. She'll have instructions, and the purser will keep close watch over her. She'll be in good hands. She turned to me. "What do you think, Mariechen? May I call you by your nick name?"

I nodded and she went on telling Gottliebe that she personally would see that I got on the train. "I'll fix her a lunch to take with her. She'll be just fine. She'll also have some money to see her through to her destination."

Gottliebe and I hugged, tears in our eyes because it had been such a short reunion for us. We hadn't seen each other for four years and now were together only a few days and a couple hours on the train. It was hard to say goodbye to Gottliebe because I knew I wouldn't see her for a long time, maybe never. War sure hurts a lot of people, separates families and scatters them all over the world.

As you might remember Gottliebe had been our mother figure for three years after our mother went to the hospital and after she died. It was an unhappy parting for us both.

"Goodbye, Mariechen, you mind them now, okay?"

That seemed all I ever heard when I said good-bye. I just stood there, tears rolling down my cheeks. I'll cry later, I thought, now I have to get my luggage into the auto and get settled for the night.

We drove to a big building. Inside it was beautifully furnished, a classic hotel from the old school. It was so grand I was sure that before the war we wouldn't have been able to touch foot in this lobby. Now, the lovely young Freulein Strauss and I would be spending the night.

We checked in and got all my papers in order. I was told to sit and wait in a big easy chair. I fell asleep and was awakened by Freulein Strauss and an elderly lady in a Red Cross uniform. She was very kind and told Freulein Strauss to take me to my room and get me some dinner. I was to share a room with two other girls. They were already fast asleep when we arrived. I put on my nightgown and got ready for bed. Freulein Strauss brought me some supper, Bratwurst and potato salad and apple cider and a piece of apple Strudel for dessert. I finished, set the tray outside and fell asleep almost before I hit the pillow.

I had unusual dreams, all jumbled up, and as if reliving all that happened in my travels the last few years. First I was little again, running and running, trying to get away from something or someone. Next I was in Runn with my father and sisters, my mother laughing and singing to me. Then everything changed again. I was in a dark place and everyone was wearing dark clothes and crying, and when I woke tears were rolling down my cheeks, and I felt sad.

We had to get up early to have breakfast and get to the station. Freulein Strauss took charge. She had us up and dressed and ready within the hour. A continental breakfast was served in the Dinning Hall and it was great, lots of different pastries, hot milk and fruit. It was delicious, and I took extra for the trip.

Maria, Gypsy Princess

We arrived at the station in plenty of time and were in luck. The train was already there so we boarded right away. Freulein Strauss got me settled in and stayed a little while. She gave the purser some last minute instructions, then came back to say goodbye and tell me she'd sent my father a telegram to let him know I would arrive on time. She waved to me through the window as the train slowly moved out of the station.

I settled back into my seat, closed my eyes, letting everything sink in. Here I was again taking another trip into the unknown. Life had thrown me a lot of curves in the last eight years, and I was sure a lot more were to come before I finished my travels.

The chukka, chukka lulled me to sleep and back into my dream world. This time my dreams seemed to take me to the future. I dreamed about my father, how we would fall into each other's arms, and it felt good. When I awoke the conductor had just come to click our tickets. He winked at me as he left. I noticed there were only three other people in the compartment, an elderly couple and a young lad about my age, maybe a couple of years older.

The boy addressed me with an Austrian accent I had a hard time understanding. It sounded as if he was asking where I was going and where I came from. I answered and let it go. It was almost noon and I was getting hungry but didn't want to take my food down from the shelf first. So I sat in my corner looking out the window, watching the countryside fly by. The area around Salzburg was beautiful and peaceful. Luckily, it wasn't destroyed by bombs. The war wasn't fought here, which sure made a difference in the countryside.

I was thinking of my father and sister, wondering how they had changed and what they would think of me. I had changed a lot too. I really didn't look forward to seeing Mutti again. She was one reason I left Runn in the first place. However, I looked forward to meeting my new sister, Monika, three years old now. I also missed my sister, Vickie, who I loved dearly and hadn't seen in years. My stepbrother, Kurt, and I always got along great. It'd be nice to see him again.

Alma and Mathias and their two kids lived in Baden near Vienna. They wandered around Yugoslavia and Austria for five months before they settled in Baden, so I was told later by Alma. I don't know that whole story, exactly where their wanderings took them and why five months. I've had a hard time getting anything out of my sisters. I don't try anymore.

When I came back from my musings, the couple across was eating, so I took down the bundle Freulein had packed for me and it was a pleasantly surprised. Chicken, cheese, dark bread, liverwurst and all kinds of yummy pastries I loved and also "most" to drink. Most is like apple cider, fresh and tasty. There were also worst with sauerkraut and hard rolls for my dinner. At least I wouldn't starve on this trip.

I noticed the boy named Fritz wasn't eating so I offered him half of my liverwurst sandwich. At first he shook his head, "Nein, nein," but I insisted. I could tell he was hungry. He inhaled it so fast I hardly had time to turn around before it was gone. The older couple noticed too, because the lady gave him some fruit and pastries. He was very grateful. He said he had run out of food and money the night before but would be home in a couple of hours and would be all right.

Good deed done, food put away, I stood and went to the bathroom, then wandered around the train to stretch my legs and chat with other passengers. Most were Austrians and wanted to know my story. I wasn't as shy as I used to be, so was glad to tell it. Of course, in those days everyone in Europe had a story to tell.

Father, indeed, was waiting for me in Friesach, and it was such joy to lay my eyes on him that at first I couldn't move. My spirits were at such high pitch, I felt feverish. It had been such a long wait to see my father again. I thought this day would never come. I'd been looking forward to this moment and seeing it in my dreams for years. All I wanted was to throw myself at Vati, and what did I do? I stood there, unable to budge an inch. When I finally came to my senses, I was on the bottom step of the train and Vati was right in front of me with outstretched arms. Without another thought, I fell into his arms sighing with relief. Vati's arms felt wonderful and his closeness almost made me dizzy.

His cheek close to mine felt familiar and even his stubbly face felt good. I snuggled my head into his shoulder and let my tears flow. He lifted me off the platform and set me down. "You sure have grown," he said. "You're a young lady now. Where did my little Mariechen go?"

"Vati, she's still here. In my heart I'll always be your little Mariechen!"

I was really; really happy Vati came to pick me up all by him self, because I didn't want anything or anyone to interfere with our reunion. I wanted to revel in my joy as long as possible. I was grateful just being alive and in my father's presence again.

When we got home, Monika turned out to be shy and spoiled and Mutti doted on her. "Moni," that's what we called her, wouldn't let Mutti out of her sight, she hung onto Mutti's apron string and follow wherever she went. Mutti seemed mellower than I remembered, and we had a pleasant reunion and gave me a warm hug. I had brought Moni a little doll and presented it to her, but she was so shy she hid behind Mutti, peeking around her back, a finger in her mouth. Her big brown eyes, so like mine, were round saucers full of anxiety. Vati finally coaxed her out from behind Mutti, and she accepted

Maria, Gypsy Princess

my gift and said, "Danke." But she wouldn't let me hug her yet. I think being carried so much made her anxious and shy.

It was too early to tell how well Mutti and I would get on. We'd have to give it some time and see what developed between us.

Kurt hadn't changed much, just taller, the same smart aleck as before. He came and hugged me and swung me around. "I am glad you're back, little sister. I missed you."

That was sweet and I hugged him back. "I missed all of you, too."

I was sorry Vicki wasn't home to greet me, but she was working in another town and wouldn't be home until the weekend. Neither would Helga. They both worked for the same firm in Klagenfurt. Renate had a job in the Alps in Tirol, too far away to come home on a weekend. She only came home once a month if she had enough free time.

I could hardly wait for the weekend. I missed Vickie so much. We had a great reunion, hugged and she held my face in he hands and kissed me, then held me away from her and started to cry. I snuggled back into her arms and cried too.

When Helga came she patted my head and said, "You sure have grown a lot. How old are you now?"

"I am twelve," I said. "It's nice to see you too."

I asked Vati when we were going to the USA, and he told me the papers were in the works, but it would be at least two years or so before we would leave. I was glad I didn't have to go to school right of away and had enough time to get to know everyone again. Vickie and I spend many hours together that weekend, mostly talking about the old days. We also talked a little about the war. She told how they ran from the Yugoslavian army, and I told her about fleeing from the Russians. It was hard for me when Vickie went back to work.

I made friends that summer. One was Frieda Graus. We became best friends. In the fall I had to start school and dreaded it a little because I would have to go into a lower class with kids two years younger again. Nothing I could do but forge ahead and study as hard as I could to catch up. I was lucky and made friends easily and had no problem fitting in. I always liked sports and was competitive. Fokker ball was my game, like touch ball in this country.

Friesach was about five miles away from our little village of Graffendorf, and I walked to school and back every day. There was a small creek with a little bridge, and I would stop there and watch the fish German brown trout were swim under it. I thought how great it would be if Vati and I could come here alone fishing. So I asked if he could take me fishing after his Saturday shopping in Friesach.

Maria Reule Woelfl

He indeed said yes, but Mutti said we couldn't go unless we took Moni. "Oh no," I grumbled, "I want to spent a few hours just with Vati. Do we have to take her?"

"Its okay, Mariechen," Vati said. "We'll still have a good time. Just bring some of her favorite toys. She'll sit and play." We did have a great time and we caught enough trout to feed all of us for supper.

We shared a four-room house with a farmhand who worked for the lady who owned the house and all the land around. She was a grand old dame who owned a lot of land in the area. There was a big garden with every sort of fruit tree you can think of. All we had to do was go out the front door and there was fresh fruit just for the picking. We also had to pick them up from the ground for Frau Foxx and they made "Most", a drink everyone enjoyed. That was her name.

She had a big house and was well known in the village. They also distilling, the rotted fruit into Kirshwasser (plum Schnapps) and all kinds of liqueurs for their own use and to sell and sold fresh fruit in the market place too.

She was a nice old lady and really liked Kurt so we were often invited to the great house, sometimes for Sunday dinner. Frau Foxx had a daughter and a two-year-old grandson. The boy, Karl, was conceived out of wedlock, so Frau Foxx bought her daughter, Isabella, a husband. He was an older man, very stiff and straight-laced, and he didn't belong on a farm. He only married Isabella for the money she would inherit some day. Isabella was still in love with a poor shepherd boy her mother wouldn't let her marry. The old lady was very strict and told Isabella if she didn't give up her young man, she wouldn't be welcome in her house or inherit anything. So Isabella gave him up and married without love. It sounded like one of father's fairy tales only so far the shepherd hadn't turned into a prince to take Isabella away.

My father also made Schnapps from fallen fruit. He made a stile from a big drum, and it had copper tubes spiraling down the side. We would build a fire under it and make sure it kept alive. The liquid came through the spiral tube and it would drip, drip slowly into a small pot. The only problem father had was getting enough sugar to keep the stile going.

Fall was harvest time, and Frau Foxx needed extra workers to make hay and bring the potato crop in. So we worked for her. They children only went to school a half of day because there weren't enough school rooms or teachers for all the children. So we had plenty of time to help out on the farm. I, for one, worked a couple hours in the fields in the morning, at noon I walked to school, the classes started at one. On Saturday we also worked half day turning hay in the fields. The other half, I helped Mutti with the chores.

The outhouse had to be scrubbed down every week. I also had to clean and polish all our shoes every Saturday. Kurt and I had to saw and chop wood, then stack it in a dry area. When Mutti washed clothes I helped, especially with the white bedding which had to be bleached outside by the sun just as we did in Rumania and Runn. The women didn't have an easy time of it after the war.

Most Sundays I had to look after the brat, Moni. At first it was hard to get her away from Mutti, but after she got to know me she and I got along great. As you can tell, I didn't have much free time. I thought things would get better when I finally came home, and I wouldn't have to work all the time and take care of children, but no such luck.

Every once in a while I would rebel and take off. My best friend had moved away so I took it into my head to go visit her in a town twenty miles away. I just took my father's bicycle one Sunday afternoon and rode to my friend's village without asking anyone or telling them where I was going. It took about three hours to get there and after arrival in town, I had to ask quite a few people on the streets if they knew Frieda Graus. Most of them shook their heads. I finally found the right person and was shown where she lived. Alas she wasn't even home. Her mother told me she went to visit her grandparents in the next village. So I had made the long trip for nothing and knew I would really get it for taking off when I was supposed to watch Monika when I got home. Now my punishment was more work. I thought I had a lot to do before, but now it was worse. For a month I had to stay close to home every day, and Mutti always found something for me to do.

I missed Frieda. She was fun to be with and we used to spend all our free time together. Frieda was a Catholic and I was Lutheran, and my folks didn't want me to associate with Catholics. But I didn't care. We were best friends, and I would play with her and be with her as often as I could.

The first Christmas in Graffendorf was rather sad. We didn't have many ornaments and also not much room for a tree. The main room was not very big, and to top it all off it had two beds in it, also the cooking stove, a table with two benches and a big chair where Vati always sat. Plus there was a small cabinet for the dishes in one corner. There was not room for a big tree, so we put a small one on a little round table between the beds. There also was a smaller room it was very cozy with wall to wall beds, only enough room to squeeze through where Vickie, Helga and I slept when they were home. During the week, Kurt and I and sometimes Moni slept in that room, so Mutti and Vati had some privacy.

A third little cubicle of a room was used for storing food, and it was built of stone and was very cold. Kurt slept there when Helga and Vickie were home. He didn't like that at all. It was okay in summer, but in winter when it was below zero outside he froze his buns off in that room. So in the winter we all had to bunk together, like it or not.

Maria Reule Woelfl

Before my friend Frieda moved to another town, Kurt and I went to Midnight Mass with her on Christmas Eve at her church and it was wonderful. I knew all about Jesus and the story of "His birth," because we had celebrated and reenacted the story when we lived in Rumania.

They, reenacted it in their church, and it was beautiful. It might have been because it was midnight, and I was to be home in bed that it was more special. I was glad we had a chance to go with Frieda that year because the next Christmas she and her parents had moved away.

The only thing I didn't like about the church was, we had to walk trough the cemetery at night, and Kurt was such a stinker he hid behind a headstone and scared us as we passed. I think the whole village heard us screaming as we ran down the street. But I did get even with Kurt later, when the time was right.

It was now early fall in 1949, and nothing much was changing in our lives. One Saturday Helga and Vickie entered a swimming event and I went to watch them dive and swim laps. Helga did very well, but Vickie had cramps and didn't finish. She was very disappointed but still had a great time at the meet. After they finished their competition they went dancing. They put a dance floor right next to the swimming area and all the people danced. I tagged along for awhile, but they didn't want me to bother them. They wanted to be with their boyfriends, not their little sister. I had permission to watch them for a couple hours, but I was to be home by suppertime before it got dark.

I had such good time I forgot. It was already getting dark, and I knew I stayed too long. I couldn't find the girls or Kurt so I had to go home by myself. I was a little scared to walk the three miles in the dark and pass through a tall cornfield. The height made it scary when it rustled. I started running and singing as loud as I could and was out of breath by the time I came out the other side, but I still kept running until I was almost home.

The house was dark, and I thought Vati and Mutti were asleep, but no such luck. Father heard me come in and was very angry. I had never seen him so upset.

"Do you realize how worried I've been? You are not old enough to stay out so late."

"But, but Vati," I stuttered, "I was with Vickie, Helga and Kurt."

"Where are they then?" he asked, "I don't see any of them with you."

"They left me and I had to come home alone and I was scared of the dark."

"You were supposed to be home way before dark, remember? You had only permission to stay a few hours and to be home before dinner, right?"

"Yes, Vati. I am sorry."

"Sorry isn't good enough. Now get to bed. I'll figure out a punishment tomorrow. It is too late tonight. Good night, Maria."

I tried to give him a hug, but he turned, went back to the other room and closed the door. I really did it this time, I thought. I knew when Vati called me Maria he was really upset. I had a hard time falling asleep because I had hurt my father, one thing I never wanted to do. I loved him way too much for that. I was dreading tomorrow. I knew Mutti would get in the middle of it and make it worse.

Vati didn't say a thing at breakfast or all day, and I was worried. It was like when you lay awake at night and hear one shoe drop and wait for the second to fall. I was on pins and needles waiting for Vati to tell me what my punishment would be.

It was a whole week before Vati told me. He sat me down and spoke quietly.

"Now, Maria, I thought about it and came up with your punishment. Remember you asked me if you could go visit your friend Frieda the weekend before school starts, and I said yes? Well, the answer is no. Now you have to stay home." He held up his hand. "Pasta." (Enough). "I don't want to hear any argument from you. Next time I am sure you'll mind me and do what you're told." Then he got up and walked away.

The punishment hurt more than if Vati had given me a spanking, which he had never done. When my father made up his mind about something he never changed it.

School started and things were going smoothly without me having any mishaps. Doing my chores before and after school, feeding the rabbits - we had six bins of them and three were going to have babies soon. I was engrossed with them and wanted to be there when the babies came.

I loved my rabbits. Although they were being raised for food, I still loved to be with them and feed them. I also talked to them and took care of them as if they were my own children. Sometimes when I cleaned their cages one would get out and I had to chase it all over the yard to catch it and put it back in the pen. We also sold rabbits to other people because in those days food was scarce and so was money.

In the fall we kids from the village would go on hikes in the woods and pick black and blueberries and hazelnuts, also mushrooms. They were mostly button mushrooms because some of the others were poisonous, and if you picked the wrong ones and ate them you could die.

The Austrian countryside was really beautiful. We would climb high on top of a hill and look down the other side. As far as you could see was a beautiful valley with a stream running through it, green and peaceful with sheep grazing below and a shepherd dozing in the sun while sheep dogs ran around keeping the sheep in line.

When we were up there I always wished I had a camera so I could capture the beauty of it all. The shepherds and sometimes even their families would live there in a little one-room hut. They lived off the land and some had never seen outsiders and never left their valley. Their kids didn't go to school and couldn't read or write. It must've been a very lonely life, but if you don't know anything else, what would you miss?

We went there quite often just to enjoy the view, but we never went down to the valley because we didn't want to disturb the people who lived there.

October Fest was not too far away, and I was happy because Vickie and Helga were coming home to spend it with us. Oktoberfest was huge in Austria and everyone went way out celebrating it. There was a Guesthouse not far from where we lived which had a big yard and people came from near and far to celebrate there.

It sometimes lasted three days, starting Friday at noon and ending late Sunday evening. There was so much food you couldn't eat or even taste all of it, also barrels of wine and beer flowed freely and everyone danced and enjoyed themselves.

In the winter we went up the same hill and skied and sledded down. We had a grand time and snow fights too. I used my skis to get to school, easier than walking. It was a long, cold winter, and we were all glad when spring came and the birds were out singing again.

March came and I was fourteen years old, a young lady, but still a tomboy at heart. On my birthday nothing special happened, but I was happy because I didn't have to do any chores that day. March 8th must have fallen on a Saturday, because I know there wasn't any school that day, so I took advantage of that, no shoes to clean, no wood to saw or water to carry. The best part, I didn't have to take care of Moni.

I washed my hair and it happened to be a nice day so I went outside and put a blanket on a pile of straw and lay there, spreading my beautiful auburn hair out to dry. The sun was warm on my face, and I closed my eyes and enjoyed the warm spring weather. Birds were chirping away and there was a wonderful peace around me. What a great way to spend one's birthday, no one to tell you what to do or where to go. Just lying in the sun day dreaming of better things yet to come. I felt I was in heaven or close to it. A day would come where no one could order me around. I looked forward to that. It gave me peace.

I lay there thinking and dozing for quite awhile and when I got hungry, I went into the kitchen to ask Mutti for something to eat, but there wasn't a soul around. I fixed myself some lunch, braided my hair and went outside and wandered around seeing if I could find a friend to spend time with. I strolled down the street and came upon two girl friends. One was carrying a basket covered with a towel, and she told me she was taking it to her grandma on a farm a few kilometers away. She asked if I'd like to come along.

So the three of us went to grandmother's house, and Greta asked why I was out and about because she knew I always had a lot of chores on Saturday.

"Well, it's my birthday today, and my folks gave me the day off for a present."

She and Ursula said, "Great, happy birthday."

"I know my grandma will fix us a treat," Greta said. Her grandmother was a wonderful cook and baker.

It took us over an hour to get there, but it was worth it because Greta's grandma indeed laid out a wonderful spread for us, all kinds of meats, breads and pastries, also tea. We were there a couple of hours when I said, "We'd better go back now. I didn't tell anyone where I was going."

We thanked our hostess and she was so generous she gave us some goodies to take home.

When I came home, Mutti was in the kitchen fixing dinner. She looked up and asked if I had a nice day.

"Yes, I went with Greta to visit her Grandma, and here are some goodies she gave me to bring home."

"Wonderful, we can have some for dessert"

"Oh, I thought you made me a cake for my birthday."

"I did, but it's always nice to have extra goodies."

I really wasn't hungry yet so I said I hope we wouldn't eat too soon, I'd had a big lunch. "By the way, where are Vati, Moni and Kurt?"

"Moni is taking a nap. We walked quite a ways and she was tired, and Vati went to visit a friend. He should be back within the hour. I don't know where Kurt is. He took his bicycle and left a few hours ago to visit someone. He should be back for supper."

I asked if she needed any help, but she waved me off. "No, it's your birthday. Go do what you want."

I left her and wandered up to the big house to say halo to Frau Foxx. She asked me in and said how nice it was for me to come see her. We sat down and she poured us a glass of wine. She raised her glass. "To you," she said, "I understand today is your birthday."

I was astounded she knew, also flattered that she remembered it. We drank in silence for awhile, and then she asked my age.

"Fourteen," I told her.

She nodded. "A good age, a good age. I wish I was fourteen again!"

We chit chatted a little longer and I said my farewells, and at the door she gave me two Schillings. That made my day. So far it had been great. I walked home to be with my family.

Vati was home and greeted me with a big hug and asked if I'd had a nice day so far. I told him, yes, and enlightened him about my day.

When Kurt came home we had dinner and ate the cake Mutti made for me, and they all sang happy birthday. They all gave me gifts they made themselves. Mutti gave me an embroidered hanky, Vati made me clogs, Kurt gave me a comb and Moni drew me a picture she said was the family of rabbits. All and all, I had a great day!

Spring went slowly and school was not too exciting for me. I caught up a little so I was only one year older than the kids in my class, but they seemed like babies compared to me with my world travels. The school had a policy that children couldn't go to a movie that was rated over sixteen only, so all the good movies I wanted to see I couldn't because of my age. An American film called "Ali Baba and the Forty Thieves" was playing, and because there was some kissing in it and the Arabian dancers showed too much flesh, we were not allowed to see it.

I asked my father if I could go and he gave his okay, so Sunday afternoon a friend and I went. Unbeknownst to us someone was there who knew we were only fourteen. Wilma and I had a great time, enjoyed the movie very much and were still talking about on the way home. The next day our teacher asked if any of us went to see the English speaking movie. No one raised a hand.

I didn't know she already knew I was there. One of the girls in my class told that her older sister had seen me there, but she only named me and not Wilma. Frau Schuler asked me directly, and I denied that I was there. She kept asking, and I shook my head no.

The girl who betrayed me stood up and said, "Maria, you were too there because my sister saw you, and the principal was there too."

Well, I had no recourse so I stood and admitted it, and said it was a great movie and my father gave me permission to go. So I didn't see what I did wrong. For not telling the truth right away, I had to go stand in the corner and had to stay there during recess.

When the class came back the teacher brought the principal with her. He addressed us about the evils of movies that corrupt young minds. My punishment was that for two days I had to come to school early the next morning with the first graders, and then still go to my own class in the afternoon.

I hated to get up so early and didn't know how to tell my folks I couldn't do my morning chores. I needed to take my lunch because it was too far to come home and get back in time for my own class. I was happy my father didn't punish me too. After all, he gave his permission.

I hated that I had to stay with the first graders. They all gawked at me and didn't quite know what to make of me the first day. The second day was better because the teacher let me help with their reading lessons, and we had fun at recess.

I was glad when summer finally came, but as usual it too went too fast, and then I had to go back to school again.

That summer Vickie came home one weekend and told us she was in love with a British solder, and he wanted to take her to England get married. We were stunned, and my father was very unhappy about it.

But you are coming to America with us," he said, "the papers are in the works and should come any day now. I forbid you to go to England." He had tears in his eyes, and he pulled out his handkerchief, blew his nose and it sounded like a trumpet.

Vickie's' eyes were also wet and so were mine.

I begged her, "You can't go. I just got back, and if we go to America we'll never see each other again."

She looked at me with sad eyes so much like mine and gave me a big hug and we stood that way for quite awhile, until Vati pulled us apart and took Vickie by the hand and pulled her out of the room

"Let's go for a walk," he said. I followed behind them, but Vati held up his hand. "Just Vickie and me this time."

It seemed a long time until they returned. Vati said, "It's all settled. After all, Vickie is old enough to make up her own mind, and if she loves this guy we can't stand in her way."

She promised to bring her Ed Brett home the following weekend so we could meet him. They had to leave real soon because he was being shipped home in a couple of months and she needed to get her papers in order.

Helga was also there and said Ed was her boyfriend first but she didn't want him so he went to Vickie. "I could have had him if I really wanted him," she said.

I just gave her a dirty look and went over and kissed Vickie and wished her well.

It was a sad day when Vickie left for England, but Ed seemed to be a nice fellow even though we couldn't understand a word he was saying. I could see he loved Vickie by the way he looked at her when she wasn't looking.

Now our family would be even farther apart than before. All the sisters were in different countries; Anna in Rumania, Emma in East Germany, Gottliebe in West Germany, Alma here in Austria, but so far away I hadn't seen her yet. And now Vickie would be in Britain, and when we left for the

USA we most likely wouldn't see each for years, if ever. Our family didn't seem a family any more. What war did to our family and so many others was a crime.

It was a sad summer for me, and I could tell Vati was taking Vickie's leaving very hard too.

Vickie before leaving for England

One day late that fall I was walking home from school and decided to hitch a ride home. A big truck was parked in front of a cloister, the driver delivering something to the nuns. I climbed onto the back of the truck and hid. When the driver came back he just jumped in and took off, driving at first thirty to forty kilometers an hour and maybe even up to fifty on the highway. Since he didn't know I was there, he didn't slow down when it came time for me to get off. Luckily, he had slowed a little because a cross road and house were coming up.

I climbed down, hung on the back and let myself down until my feet brushed the asphalt, then let go. Of course, I hit the pavement with force, knocking my head hard on the asphalt and passing out. I don't know how long I lay there. When I came to, I rolled myself off the middle of the road onto the shoulder into the grass and passed out again.

I lay there until someone came by riding his bicycle on the way home. He spotted me as he rode by and stopped to check me out. He put his jacket under my head, and then went for help. He worked in a factory not far away, and that's where he went to get his boss who had an auto. They came back and the boss took me to the doctor in Friesach. That's where I had just hitched a ride from. I woke up long enough to tell them my name. Luckily, the man who found me knew my father and went on his bicycle to tell him where I was.

Maria, Gypsy Princess

There was only one doctor in Friesach. My father rode his bicycle all the way to Friesach. Needless to say, he wasn't too happy about it. I was one lucky girl. I just had some scratches and bruises and a cut over my right eye. My right eardrum was damaged. Otherwise I was okay. Again God and the angels were with me.

Vati was happy I wasn't hurt too badly, but now I had to await another punishment I knew was coming. I had to stay home from school a few days to heal. When I went back everyone was happy to see me and glad I wasn't in worse shape. A week or so later our teacher announced the class would take an Ausflug to the Tyrolean Alps. All we needed was twenty Schillings and our parents' permission. I was all excited because I would see my sister Renate again, but this time I would only say hi to her and then go with the rest of the group and have fun skiing and sledding. On last year's trip I stayed behind with Renate at the Chelae where she worked. So I didn't get to see much and it was boring to just sit and wait for Renate to get off work.

I was bubbling over with excitement when I told Vati and Mutti about the trip. They listened quietly until I finished, then my father said, "How much will it cost?"

"Oh Vati, not so much, I just need twenty Shillings."

Vati walked back and forth with a stern face saying nothing for a good while, and when he stopped he said, "Sorry, Maria, because I had to pay the doctor, we don't have the extra money for your trip. This shall be your punishment for being so reckless. How do I know you wouldn't get hurt again roaming around on the top of the Alps?"

Oh, that really hurt, more than the fall from the truck. "Please, I'll work extra hard, and I am sure Frau Foxx would give me an advance. I could work it off in no time."

"No, I'm sorry, my mind is made up. You can't go, and that's that.

Unless I got the money from somewhere else, I knew Vati would not change his mind. I somehow had to figure a way to get that twenty Schillings. The next day at school I told my teacher what father had said. "Oh, I'm so sorry," she said. "Are you sure he won't change his mind?"

"No, not my father. When it comes to money, he never has."

"Don't despair," she said, "today is Friday. I'll think on it and see if I can't come up with something to help you by Monday."

I was in anguish all weekend and prayed Frau Schuler would come up with a good plan. When Monday came I could hardly wait to get to school. I wanted to talk to her ahead of time, but the bell sounded and I had to go into class with everyone else. We went on with our lessons and it was an excruciating day for me. Just before the bell for recess she asked the class if they would help me so I could go on the ski trip too. They all raised their hands and said, "Yes, yes, yes." She had come up with a plan. She said, "There are twenty-one people in this class, and if we all come up with one extra Shilling Maria shall have enough money to go with us, okay?" They were all enthusiastic and started talking at the same time.

Frau Schuler had to quiet everyone down before she could go on. "It all hangs on if your parents say yes to this plan, so you must talk to your parents before Maria says anything or bring it up with her father, alright?" So the next day it was decided that everyone would ask for the extra money, and then we'd see if I could go.

All the parents said yes and I was delighted. Now all I had to do was sell the idea too Vati. Not an easy task. I didn't quite know how to go about it. That evening at supper I brought it up and told them how great everyone was to give me the money so I could go too. They listened, as a matter of fact it seemed too quiet to my thinking. After I finished my spiel, I looked first at Mutti with pleading eyes and then to my father. Vati didn't look happy. He was frowning, and a sinking feeling came over me. Without him saying a word, I knew the answer was "No."

"I am sorry, Maria," said Vati, "I can't let you go. For one thing, I don't accept charity, and how do I know you wouldn't get hurt up there? So it's a definite no. "Das ist schuss, ich will nicht mar von diesem horen," he said. (Now don't bring the matter up again).

Well, that was the end of it, but I knew there would soon be other trip far more exciting than the Alps. Three years earlier Father had started preparing our papers to go to America, and they were finally coming through. Vati received a letter from the Austrian Consulate that everything was in order. All we had to do now was take a train to Salzburg, get our visas and sign the papers. Then we would be ready to leave for the U.S.A.

Vati, Mutti, Kurt, Monica and I, were the only ones from our family who would travel to America. My sisters all stayed in Europe. A few years later my stepsisters, Helga and Renate, were sponsored by a lady named Mackenzie. I went to work for Mrs. Mackenzie two years after we arrived in Jamestown, North Dakota. But that comes later.

Chapter 16

It was a long cold winter and there were no more mishaps. I guess I was growing up and getting used to doing what I was told. I had fended for myself and taken care of three young children. I had made many decisions on my own. Although I'd had to listen to Emma, it was different now.

March came and I turned fifteen. I was a young woman now because just a couple of weeks after my birthday my period started. I thought I was bleeding to death. I was sitting in the outhouse when it happened and didn't know what to do. I had nothing to use. There were only old newspapers so I folded a piece, put it into my underpants and ran to the house, shaking and crying.

Mutti asked what was wrong with me. When I told her, she said, "Oh, there's nothing to worry about. It happens to all girls around your age, some even younger." She went to a box where some old clothes were kept, tore a piece from a shirt and told me to put it in my pants. "If you need more just tear more strips, anything from the pile. Wash the piece you're using, also your pants and hang them on the line. Use cold water or it won't come out. You'll have your period for three to five days every month from now on." She added, "I am still angry with Vickie because she used one of my good handkerchiefs when she first had the curse."

Mutti didn't explain anything more, and I had no idea how to ask what it all meant. A few days later I was scrubbing the hall floor and heard Mutti and a neighbor talking in the kitchen. They were loud enough for me to hear everything.

"When a girl starts her period she has to be very careful or she'll be with child," the neighbor said.

"Yes," Mutti said, "they have to stay away from boys to be safe."

The whole conversation was for my benefit. Of course, I had no idea what they meant. Stay away from boys? I couldn't even talk to one or hold hands? Or maybe they meant don't kiss a boy! I really didn't know. I'd have to ask someone else.

Oh how I wished Vickie was still with us. I missed her so much. I couldn't talk to Helga. She scared me. Maybe Kurt would tell me. I knew he was smitten with me because lately he'd been trying to feel me up and give me little kisses. One time he pulled me close and gave me a big, sloppy kiss right on the mouth. I hated it. Ich, it was awful. If kisses were like that, I didn't like them at all.

I did ask him, and he told me it wasn't from touching or kissing. You had to do much more, but he didn't explain what. I was so ignorant about it all. I still thought babies came from storks, as I was told when I was little.

That spring I was going to be confirmed. I had to study Bible scriptures and learn about the Apostles. As I wrote before, because Austria was mostly Catholic, we had a minister who came to our area only once a month. There were only a few Lutherans Churches in the area. The Lutheran church was in the city of Villach. Villach is a lovely small city about 150 kilometers from where we lived and the state capital of Kärnten. We had to take a train there because we had no auto. No one in the family could drive anyway, so we had to ask someone else to drive us.

I took the train to Villach two days before the confirmation and stayed with the Minister and his wife. Two other girls came from out of town, we all shared a room, and it was great fun. We took some classes from Frau Vogel, the Minister's wife. She taught us about God, to read and learn from the New Testament and the wonders of Jesus' life. It was all about His good deeds and loving ways, healing the sick just by touching them. If they believed they were healed right on the spot. How amazing he was, and having to die so young. That saddened me. Why would they kill someone who did so many wonderful, loving deeds, and gave His life for others? I always believed, if we followed Jesus' teachings and loved one another as He loved us, we would have no war or strife.

On Sunday all the families of the young ladies came for the confirmation. It was a beautiful ceremony, and all of the mothers sniffed out loud and the fathers blew their noses noisily. Even my father had shiny eyes when I kissed him after the service.

We couldn't afford a new dress so Mutti revamped one of her old dresses. It was a dark blue crepe, too short for me, so Vati bought a piece of material the same color and Mutti put the strip of material in the middle and made a sash to go around my waist. She also made a white lace collar and trim for the cuffs, and it looked like new.

There was a reception after the service. With our help, Frau Vogel set up a long table and we put out all the goodies there before we went into church.

Maria, Gypsy Princess

It looked great and all tasted wonderful, a nice spread with assorted cheeses and sausages and delicious pastries that melted in your mouth. Each family brought something for the luncheon. They even served wine, and we were allowed to have a glass that wasn't watered down. Umm, it was tasty. We said our good byes and someone with a car drove us to the station, one family at the time. It was a great experience and something I could tell my friends about.

Our immigration papers arrived in late May, and we all took the train to Salzburg to the consulate to get them signed. They took our pictures and thumbprints. Also we had to have shots to enter the USA. Only three more weeks before we left for America we are going to a place called North Dakota. In the late 1800s my father's great uncle, Jake Reule and his family had migrated to America instead of Rumania. We were sponsored by them and would work on their farm. It was a scary thought, a completely new life, a new language to learn in a new nation. We hoped it wouldn't be too difficult.

Our emotions ran high. We didn't know what to expect from Americans. Not only the language, but new ideas, different clothes, and many other things we'd have to get used to. Yet it was exciting, a new and wonderful land. What would it offer us? Would we end up in a land of plenty, or would there only be more hard work and nothing to show for it? We'd find out soon enough.

Our good-byes were bittersweet, not only from our friends and Frau Foxx, but Helga and Renate because they could not come with us then. They really didn't want to come, so they said, but I am not to sure that was true. Both Helga and Renate came home the weekend before we left to spend time with their mother and say good bye to the rest of us. There was talk and promises to write, also hugs and kisses and crying. We exchanged small gifts too, and the next day we were off. We took the train to Salzburg, then to Paris and Le Havre to board the ship.

Salzburg is a beautiful city. We spent a day there and loved it, the Burgs and great Gashouses we just didn't have enough time to enjoy it all. It was the same in Paris. We only stayed one night and half a day, so there was only time to go to the open markets and sit and have coffee in a sidewalk café. It was all very exciting, although not pleasant because the French didn't like Germans and showed it by being disagreeable and curt.

The train to Le Havre was uneventful. Boarding the ship Le France seemed to take longer than necessary. When it dawned on us that we were really leaving Europe and sailing off to a new world. We couldn't change our minds, so we were all a little sad.

It took hours to get settled in, and felt strange to be on a big ocean liner. Our first stop was Dover, England to pick up passengers. Father hoped to get

Maria Reule Woelfl

off the ship there, because he had a gift for Vickie and wanted to say good bye to her and Ed. They came to see us off, but, alas, it wasn't to be, my Father wasn't allowed to go ashore and Vickie could not come on board. So Vati threw the watch he had bought for Vickie over the side, and thank God it landed close to her feet and not in the water.

Over fifty years later Vickie told me she still had that watch and it still worked. It was still ticking when she died in 2005.

We waved and said so long to Europe and hello America.

Chapters 17
New Land!

The only difficulty we encountered aboard ship was we didn't speak a word of English or have proper clothes to wear it didn't effect Kurt and me. That's after three days of seasickness we joined all the activities on board and we had a marvelous time.

Mutti spent the first five days on board sick in bed. When she finally felt better she had her hands full coping with five-year-old Monika. I was glad I was no longer laid up, because it was great, to eat the fabulous food served on the ship. My father only missed one meal. He said we already paid for it and there were no refunds, so we should eat every meal to get our money's worth. "Enjoy it while you can, he said, who knows what the future will bring." As if we could store it up for later. My frugal father, always practical. He hated to waste anything, especially food because for the longest time after World War II food was in short supply.

I always loved going to the movies, so while on the ship I saw my second American film, "The Jazz Singer" with Al Jolson, and I will never forget it. Al Jolson was a great entertainer and in this movie he played a colored showman in the Deep South. His face was blackened with shoe polish, and he wore white spats over his shoes. He rolled his big brown eyes around and around in his head, shuffling his feet and moving his white gloved hands side to side, singing, "Mammy." What a marvelous show.

We were in third class, so the same movie showed for three days and I saw it all three times and enjoyed it tremendously. Those were the good old days when you could sink your teeth into a plot. Sometimes Kurt and I would sneak upstairs to the second class deck and watch people dance. When they did the Bunny Hop, we'd join in. We also went to dance classes and learned some Latin steps.

Maria Reule Woelfl

Ten days after we left Le Havre we arrived in New York. Luckily, we didn't have to go through Ellis Island. Passengers didn't disembark on the Island anymore.

New York! I wanted to see The Statue of Liberty! But we were deep in the bowels of the ship and had no chance of seeing Lady Liberty. Kurt and I wanted to go up on deck, but my father stopped us. "You two better stay close, he said, I don't want to have to come looking for you when it's time to get off." We kept begging, and Vati finally relented and let us go. We took off running, afraid he would change his mind. He hollered after us "Be back in twenty minutes, we're disembarking soon.

It was difficult getting upstairs with so many people milling around, but we finally squeezed through the throng and got a whiff of fresh sea air. It was a beautiful night and the stars were out. We tried to get to the railing to spot the statue, but we must've been on the wrong side. All we saw was the dark water and the New York skyline blinking in the distance. No Lady Liberty! We were so disappointed and there wasn't time to see more.

We had to get back to disembark and the excitement was welled up in me. A new life in a land that was foreign to us and where a different language was spoken also with new and fascinating people to be met.

I wanted to be the first one off the ship, first to touch American soil. The standing and waiting was too long for me. I thought we'd never reach the gangplank. I ran ahead of everyone, and my excitement was at a fever pitch. As I moved through the human throng of people, I heard my father shout, "Mariechen, don't get so far ahead, you'll get lost." I was at the gangplank and tried to run down and off it, but the immigration people made me wait for my family. I couldn't step onto American soil without my passport anyway.

I was so close to the ramp, I saw a sign below with our name on it. "Someone is looking for us," I hollered back in German. I tried to head for the sign, but someone caught my arm and held me back. I heard my father's voice behind me, but all I could think was being first to reach the sign that said Reule on it. I was unhappy to be held back. When my family finally reached the gangplank and Father gave the immigration people our papers, I ran off the ship without looking back.

It seeming an eternity to me wiggling, through human bodies and almost getting crushed, I finally reached the spot where signs were held up. I had to step back to find the person holding ours. To my surprise, a nice looking young lady was calling our name. She didn't pronounce it correctly, but it was spelled the right way. I ran towards her, shouting voice and said, "I'm Maria Reule," but it didn't register at first because it was so noisy. I also pronounced the name the right way. But when I got close, she answered me in German. "Gutten Morgen Freulein Reule, where are your parents?"

"Right behind me," I said, but when I looked back, they were still stuck on the gangplank above. It took them another half hour to reach us.

When we were all together again I kept poking Kurt in the ribs, bragging that I was the first one off. "Stop making a nuisance of your self," Kurt said, "Stop poking me." My exuberance kept bubbling over and I could hardly stand still. My excitement was soon dampened because we had to wait for hours for customs to release our papers. We sat on a long, cold wooden bench, tired and disgruntled. My five-year-old sister Moni was the smart one. She laid her head on Mutti's lap and went fast asleep.

My head was drooping too, but I had no place to lay it. We had been sitting on this bench for two hours now. Finally customs let us go. It was four in the morning now, and we had to get to the station to catch our train, which was leaving for North Dakota at six. All in all, New York was a bust because all we saw were lights blinking in the distance. After customs released us, the same nice young lady hustled us to a shuttle. Her name was Laura and she spoke fluent German. Our train was already at the station when we arrived, and we barely made it. The all aboard called was called a few minutes after we arrived, and as soon as we were on the train, the doors clamped shut and the train started to move.

My earlier excitement left me, and all I wanted was to find a corner, curl up and sleep for days. My mind fell into the rhythm of the train, and the chukka, chukka lulled me to sleep. I had a disturbing dream, everything jumbled up, and too many faces crowding around me and they where coming from all different directions. I was trying to find my way out of a crowd and find a familiar face. Finally when I saw my mother's face but couldn't get to it, there was nothing I could hold on too. I struggled in this nightmare for a long time until I finally found my way back to reality and woke breathing hard.

I looked around and felt lost, still in the nightmare. I couldn't see my parents or my brother in the sea of strange faces. When I went to sleep they were just two rows in front, now I couldn't see them. I was struck with panic, my hands sweaty, and tears in my eyes. "Where am I?" I was on a train but where was my family? "Where are they?" I stood to look around. Sleeping bodies were everywhere, but I still couldn't spot my parents. I hurried down the aisle and back, scrutinizing all the faces. When I finally found my father, tears of joy rolled down my cheeks. He was so dear to me, the thought of losing him almost touched a new panic, but I sighed with relief when I saw them all together.

Mutti had her head on father's shoulder and Monika's head snuggled in Mutti's lap, her finger in her mouth making small sucking sounds. Kurt was sleeping a couple of rows back from my parents. I needed to go to the toilet and didn't know where it was. I stood staring at my father, hoping he'd wake up. He must have sensed my presence because his eyes opened so suddenly I was startled.

"Ah, Mariechen, how come you're awake so early?"

"Papa, I have to use the bathroom and don't know where to go."

He pointed to the back of the car, "Through the door was to the right."

So I headed that way. When I looked in the mirror, I could not believe it was me. My clothes were wrinkled and my hair a mess. My pigtails were standing out sideways, away from my ears and some hair came loose and hung straight down. I did the best I could with my appearance, but it was hopeless. I splashed water on my face, ran my hands through my hair and went back to the open seating car, a few people were already stirring, and some sat up yawning and stretching. I was hungry and wanted my parents to wake up so we could eat. I went and stood in front of them and tickled Monika. If she awoke, Mutti would give her whatever she wanted. She'd be hungry too and if she got fed so would I.

Moni awoke with a whine. "Let me be," she said, yawning.

"Come on, wake up. Aren't you hungry?"

"Yes, but I'd rather sleep." She closed her eyes again.

I bent and whispered in her ear, "I bet Mutti will give you candy after breakfast, come on wake up." She opened her eyes and there was a sparkle in them now. She was thinking of candy.

She sat up and poked Mutti in the side. "Mutti, I'm hungry."

Mutti and Vati opened their eyes. "Now, what is going on here?" Father said,

"Mariechen, what is it?"

"We're hungry."

"Oh, okay, let's have breakfast." He stood and took a little suitcase from the luggage rack, plus a basket with fruit. We didn't have much money so while on the ship Mutti had squirreled some food away. She had hoarded leftovers, and made sandwiches and kept them in the little icebox in our room she had also saved some fruit.

We had to disembarked at one o'clock in the morning so we had to put our luggage outside the cabin before early so the porter could pick it up. At midnight all we had to do was get up and get dressed. To our surprise and pleasure, the porter had left a basket full of goodies in front of our cabin for a snack. I wanted to tear it open and eat a piece of fruit, but Mutti, scolded me," No, leave that alone. We'll need it on our trip to North Dakota." That's why we had all that good food to eat now.

The train trip took five days, and it was the same routine every day. We took turns washing. I asked Mutti for a comb to tidy my hair and she also gave me a washcloth, towel and a clean blouse to put on. I looked and felt almost human again. Mutti and Monika came next and so on. After that, we all sat back and watched the landscape fly by.

It kept changing and was so different from in Europe. At first it was crowded with houses and big skyscrapers, but soon the view opened wide with miles and miles of empty land as far as you could see. It was beautiful, this new land. All too much for me to comprehend, the excitement gave me butterflies. What a glorious new world we were entering.

When I dozed off the dream of our new life was like a fairy tale. Soon we would be in North Dakota with people we had never met, everything different and new, a great change in our lives. America!!!

Jamestown, North Dakota.

After five tiresome days on the train, the Reule family arrived in North Dakota. Five days was too long to be on a train in a foreign country when none of us spoke the language.

We arrived in Jamestown on a Saturday. Uncle Jake, Aunt Dora and their oldest son Arthur with his two children were at the station to pick us up. Their youngest son David was away in a seminary studying to be a minister. We were relieved that they all spoke German. It was a whirlwind greeting of quick hellos, and then we were hustled into an auto and taken to their home. We stopped in front of a lovely, old colonial building, a big sprawling house. It had four bedrooms, a big kitchen, a den and living and dining room. The furnishings were old fashioned and stuffy, but good quality. We were shown to our assigned rooms upstairs and given time to clean up a bit before an early dinner. Mine was small but nicely furnished a girl's room. Mutti, Vati and Moni had a room across from me, and Kurt's was in the attic. My uncle and aunt's room was down the hall from Mutti and Vati's.

It was a good healthy meal of roast chicken and lots of fresh vegetables. Also apple pie and ice cream for dessert. That's something we hadn't eaten before, pie served with ice cream. I'd only had ice cream a few times in my life, at a fair. This was a real treat. Moni beamed and begged for more while Mutti tried to quiet her. "Nein, nein man muss zufrieden sein mit was man kriegt. Wir mussen doch noch etwas fur Morgen auf haben." (You have to be thankful and happy for what you have received. We have to save some or there won't be any for tomorrow). Then Moni quieted and stopped asking for more.

Aunt Dora wanted to give her more, but she said, "Nein Danke, Morgen mochte ich es wieder haben." (Thank you, but I'd like to have some more tomorrow). Monika was frugal like our father. She would save her candies

Maria Reule Woelfl

only eat one a day so they would last the whole week. She knew she would get more until Father went shopping for groceries on Saturdays.

When the meal was over I went into the kitchen to help with the dishes, but all we did was rinse and stack them. Father, Kurt and Uncle Jake went into the living room to talk about what kind of work we were to do, and what was expected of us while living and working the farm. The next day we moved to their farm. The Reule's had two sons, their oldest Arthur and his wife, with a boy six and a girl three, lived and worked their own farm.

They had two farms and they were a mile apart. Their son Arthur and his family were our neighbor. They would come over too help us, also show us what was to be done. His wife Isabel was a schoolteacher, a very lovely and kind person. She taught me how to read out of the book, named Jack and Jill. They went up the hill to fetch a pail of water, and so on. She also taught me to write a little English.

It was a hard life for all of us. We worked from dawn to dusk. Farmers' lives in the Mid West can be especially hard, raising cattle, bringing in the crop, making ends meet, but it's rewarding too. Our day started at five in the morning, milking the cows and feeding the stock even before we had breakfast.

At plowing and planting time, the workers stayed late in the fields until dark, and the same chores they did in the morning had to be done each evening too. It was basically the same as in Rumania, but here we had electricity and running water in the house. Here farmers had tractors to pull the plow instead of horses. It was all new to Mutti, she hadn't done this kind of work, neither had Kurt or I. I was too young when we farmed in Rumania before the war.

Now it was milking, feeding the animals, separating cream from the milk, putting it into cans that were taken to a dairy the next day. There was joy in watching new life develop and seeing the beauty in everything that grew. We all had our designated jobs. Life on a farm is a never-ending cycle of hard work and demands.

My uncle and aunt were Seventh-day Adventists and went to church on Saturday instead of Sunday. My father was really disappointed because they didn't eat pork, and it was his favor meat. Movies and dancing were also forbidden. There was no working on the Sabbath. Meals were prepared Friday and only warmed up on the Sabbath after we came home from church. Then food was put away, but the dishes were just rinsed and left to wash the next day. The other thing Vati didn't like was we had to go to their church and weren't allowed to worship as Lutherans. We couldn't understand any of the service anyway because it was in English, but we would have liked to learn English in the church of our choice.

Maria, Gypsy Princess

The work started early Monday morning. We milked nine cows every morning and night. The men left for the field really early and worked late into the night. Many times Mutti and I had to milk the cows by ourselves. Aunt Dora came to the farm sometimes to show us how to kill and dress the chickens to get them ready for market. First we had to shoo them into the chicken coop and catch one. Then we held them by the legs, lay it on a tree stump in the yard and chopped their heads off. They were let loose to hop all over the yard until all their blood ran out. The same thing we did in Rumania when we lived there. Of course, Mutti didn't know how because she had never killed anything. After aunt Dora let the first chicken loose and she saw the chickens hopping around she ran screaming. After the chickens were bled out they were put into a trough, and boiling water was poured over them. They were soaked to loosen the feathers so you could easily be plucked. They were cooled, dressed, washed and put in cold storage, and in a few days were taken to the market.

There was also a vegetable garden and a few fruit trees to be tended. In the spring planting started then weeding the garden, and in the fall we picked ripe vegetables and fruit for canning. Mutti and I did most of that. At harvest time it was real hectic and a lot more work for everyone. I remember a certain day when men stayed out late for threshing. They were in the fields until nine or ten o'clock at night. As long as it stayed light, they worked.

One day Mutti, Moni and I were home alone and had to milk the cows and feed the stock by ourselves. We took two pails and headed out, but we only made it to the back porch. Stepping off the porch Mutti twisted her ankle, and it swelled up twice its size in minutes. She couldn't even stand on it. It took all my strength to get her back into the house. She hobbled to the sofa and I put a pillow under her foot and a cold compress on it. I left Moni in charge of her, while I went out to try to milk nine cows all by myself.

As some of you know, it is very difficult to milk that many cows alone. I stripped each cow to take the pressure off the udders because when they fill up with milk it's very painful for them. They let you know when it builds up because they below and you have to milk them quick to relieve the pressure.

I was never so happy to see the men coming in from the fields so they could take over and finish the milking. Poor Mutti had to stay off her foot for quite awhile, which made my job even harder because I had to take over her work too. I should have been in school, but my Aunt Dora, was greedy and not a very nice person. When I asked her about school, she said Isabel would teach me all I needed to know for now because they needed me to help to pay back the money for the far. We ate a lot of chicken the year we where lived on the Reile farm. It was very difficult for us because, language barrier; and secondly we didn't have a car. Of course none of us could drive anyway. We solely depended on the Retile family for our livelihood and transportation. (Reile was their surname, changed from Reule). Aunt Dora let us know as often as she could that we totally depended on them for everything.

After a few months, the harvest was in, work slowed a bit, and it was getting cold. One November night a lot of snow fell. When we got up to milk and feed the stock we couldn't get out of the back door because too much snow was against it. Vati and Kurt had to dig us out, and it was slow going because they didn't have the right tools. The big shovel was in the barn. I still can't figure out how they finally made it to the barn to milk and feed the animals that day. It was not just a little snow it was deep, about five feet, almost over my head. There was a white blanket of the powdery stuff, and so beautiful it almost blinded you. The snow blower came later that day and cleared the main road, but we still had to shovel snow from the house to the road. Our first winter in North Dakota was not easy. The coal stove and furnace had to be fed constantly, which was Kurt's and my job. It was the longest, coldest winter we had ever known. We thought it was cold in Austria, but nothing like this. When the first blizzard hit we thought we would all die out there and they wouldn't find us until spring, frozen stiff.

The first Christmas was about the worst we ever spent in all our travels over the years. Christmas was always special for us, and even if we didn't have much to share or give to each other, we always had a tree. The Reile's didn't believe that Christ was their Savior so they didn't celebrate Christmas. They took us to their church a few days before Christmas Day and all made fun of our holiday. They had set up a small pine tree in the front of the church and all the kids went up and hung dollar bills on it, laughing. Aunt Dora even gave me and Moni dollars to hang on the tree. I didn't want to go, but she insisted, so I had to. Moni was too shy so Mutti went with her, and Mutti was almost in tears when she came back to her seat. It really hurt our feelings that they would make fun of our beliefs that way. On Christmas Eve we did put up a small tree in the living room, put some homemade decorations on it, shared a great dinner and sang some German carols. We exchanged some gifts we made ourselves. Father missed his Christmas drink and not being able to worship in our own church. Hopefully, we wouldn't have to stay here forever.

The time came a year later when father found out he had a cousin living in Jamestown, and they were Lutherans. That made him happy, someone with our beliefs who might help us leave the Reile's and get out of their clutches. In the spring of 1951 Aunt Dora found me a job with a nice family who had two little girls. My parents left the Reile's farm after two years. In 1952 they moved into a basement room with my father's cousin Emil Reule. They were a little crowded there but they made do. Now we could go to the Lutherans

Maria, Gypsy Princess

church on Sunday's. Father and Eberhard started to work for the railroad and Mutti worked for a bakery. So they slept in shift Vati and Eberhard left earlier in the morning for their job. While Mutti didn't start work until ten in the evening and worked until four in the morning. They didn't even need a baby sitter for Monica. But by the time the week end came they were all exhausted from working so many hours and not getting enough sleep. Especially Mutti she only got a few hours of rest because she had to take care of Monica when she got up. They were all really happy when they had enough money saved to buy some farmland. They bought it near Bismarck in the outskirts of the village of Driscoll. They moved there and lived in Driscoll for the winter. When the weather turned nice my father and Monica dug a hole on their land for a basement and bought a house and moved it on the hole they dug. Poor Monica was only eight years old when they did all this. She had to drive the tractor for the dig and wasn't too happy about the whole thing. But everyone had to do their bit in those days.

I liked my new job the Olson's were great to me. Their oldest girl was Mary was seven and her sister, Jane, was five. They were real sweet kids and taught me a lot. They helped me understand English a little better. When I didn't understand something they would show me what they wanted and tell me its name until I understood the word.

When it came to speaking English that was another story. It took me much longer to speak than to understand. I was with the Olson family a year, one of the nicest times I spent in my new country. Edie's and Al Olson treated me like family, although I worked hard every day, cooking, cleaning, washing clothes and ironing, also taking care of the two girls while Edie was at work. I was happy there. Al Olson was a salesman, and he traveled all of the time. He wore a white starched shirt every day of the week, and I had to wash and iron them. I also had to wash and iron the fluffy dresses the girls wore to school and Edie white starched blouses she wore at work. Their clothes kept me busy all the time.

Edie worked in the Jamestown Hotel's café, while I took care of the girls. When they came home for lunch, I had to make it for them. I also cooked the evening meal or at least started it before Edie came home. At lunchtime the first day, the girls asked me to make them a peanut butter and jelly sandwich. Of course, I had no idea what they were taking about. So they took down a loaf of Wonder bread, jars of peanut butter and jelly and showed me how to put the sandwich together. That's how I learned how to do a lot of things, by show and tell.

They always explained what they did and what was in it and had me pronounce all the words and then repeat them. They made sure I pronounced them correctly. That's how little by little I learned English. All the Olson's and

I became great friends. They taught me enough English so I could go out and get another job when I left their family. I ate with them and at night after the girls were in bed they let me watch TV with them.

Dean Martin and Jerry Lewis were a big hit in 1951. I enjoyed their antics immensely and couldn't get enough of them. We watched their show every week, and I got very good imitating them both. I would entertain Edie and Al, and their friends when they had a party. I had them rolling on the floor with laughter. I'd take both parts, singing like Dean, then like Jerry acting an idiot with his whinny voice and funny walk. I wish I had bottled that. Too bad the tape recorder wasn't invented yet because I would have had my own TV show, maybe a whole career. Hindsight doesn't put money in the bank.

Edie was very kind to me and taught me about being a woman. She bought me a bra. I didn't think I needed one yet because my breasts were round and firm. I actually didn't wear one until I was eighteen or so. My wages were $15.00 a week, and from that I was allowed to keep 75 cents. The rest went to my folks to pay back the money we owed my uncle for bringing us to America. Sunday, my day off, after church I'd go to three movies. At noon it was a Walt Disney film, at 3:00 a cowboy movie, and in between I had just enough money for French fries. Then I saw a romance flick in the evening. The movies also helped me learn better English.

After I'd been working for the Olson's about a year, Edie got pregnant and had to stay home and off her feet. The doctor told her to stay in bed as much as possible or she would lose the baby. She'd had a miscarriage before so this time she was to be very careful and take it easy.

Now that Edie couldn't work, they didn't have money to pay me so had to let me go. It was a sad parting, but we stayed friends until they moved away in 1954 and I lost touch with them. Edie didn't carry the baby full term after all. She miscarried after four months and they decided not to try to have more children after that.

Chapter 18

It was now 1952 and a warm spring day when I stepped out onto the porch I marveled at the clear blue sky. It had been a long cold winter, and it felt good just to stand in the warm sun and let it soak into my bones. I stood gazing up for a few minutes, letting the sun caress my face. Then I bent down to smell the roses climbing up the porch columns. "Ah." I inhaled the sweet scent. As I stepped off the porch and looked back, I knew I would soon have to leave this house. I had lived here over a year and it was like home to me now. I hated to think of leaving and trying to find another place to live.

Too soon to worry about it, I thought. I'll think of it tomorrow. I cleared my mind of it and started towards town. I loved the old houses on this street. I wished I had been born in one of these houses and grown up here. The house I'd been living in was a two story white colonial with a big front porch and a smaller one in back. A huge old oak tree stood in the middle of the front yard. In the back, an old swing was still attached to a similar tree. It swayed in the breeze, waiting for the next generation of children to swing there.

I could hear their laughter singing in my ears. "Higher, Mama, higher!" I saw them flying high, their little legs reaching towards the sky.

I loved to sit on that swing and sway to and fro. Many times, I sat there wishing and wondering what the future would bring for me. How I'd love to own one of these old houses some day. I saw myself pushing my kids on a swing, a loving man beside me and two or three children running and playing in the yard, laughing and having fun. Maybe some day, but for now it was just a dream.

I came back to reality. I was on my way to work. I'd started a job in the Moline Café. Today I would be bus-girl and clear and set the tables for the waitresses. As soon as I spoke better English, Mrs. Mack promised I would be a waitress too.

The house wasn't as big inside as it looked from the outside. The first floor consisted of a living and dining area and a den. A small kitchen and toilet were behind the kitchen. The furnishings were old and bulky. An upright piano stood just inside the front door and a big window looked out at the front yard. On the other wall was a big stuffed couch, a square oak table and lamp. The coffee table had some magazines and a deck of playing cards on it. The cards were Mrs. Mack's, the lady I work for. When she was at home she usually sat there playing solitary. She taught me how to play too.

Mr.'s Mack's sister, Dora, came to live with the family for a while and she was kind to me and taught me to play the piano, and I learned to play some duets with her.

When you entered the house the first thing you saw was the staircase to the second floor. There were four bedrooms upstairs, two in front and two in the middle on each side of the hallway. A bathroom with a tub was in the back and a staircase down to the kitchen. I slept in the smallest bedroom in front. The other front bedroom belonged to the Mackenzie's daughter, Mary, who was away at college. The room I was using belonged to their son, Charles, who was in the Marines. Their oldest son, David, was married with two kids and lived in town. I didn't know him or his wife very well.

Mr. and Mrs. Mack slept in separate bedrooms and were total opposites. It's a mystery how they got together in the first place and managed to have three children. Mrs. Mack, as we called her, was loving and kind, a motherly type always helping someone in need. She had brown eyes, a hooked nose and a dark complexion. She dyed her own hair and you could smell the Helena dye she used before you saw her, but no one cared because she was so kind to everyone. The old fashioned clothes she wore always hung loose on her big frame. I thought she looked much older than she was, but I could be wrong because I had no idea how old she really was and I doubt anyone else knew either.

On the other hand, Mr. Mack was just the opposite, tall, straight and wiry with watery blue-gray eyes, silver hair and a skinny pinched nose. He rarely smiled or even talked to you.

Charles, their youngest son, was serving a four year stint in the Korean war. He was a Marine. What a handsome, proud young man he was! When he was home on a furlough for the holidays, I had a crush on him. Although he was way too old for me, twenty-five and I only sixteen, still I couldn't help falling for him.

A few days before Christmas the doorbell rang and when I answered it, he stood there big as life, strong and virile in his dashing uniform. I almost swooned at the sight of him.

"Who are you?" he said.

I just stood there like a dummy frozen to the floor and couldn't utter a sound. I had forgotten my English, maybe my German too!

"Well, the cat's got your tongue. Speak up, girl. Is the family home? Where's my mother?"

"Oh," I muttered when I finally found my tongue, and I said, Niemen ist zuhouse, deine Mutter ist im Kaffe Haus."

"Speak English, girl, I can't understand a word you're spouting."

"Oh, I am so, so sorry, you must be Charles. Your mother is at the Café Moline."

"Okay, okay, but you still haven't told me your name and what you're doing here."

"I'm Maria Reule, and I work for your family in the house," I said shyly.

Without another word he picked up his duffel bag and ran up the stairs taking two steps at a time. He disappeared into the room I'd been using the last few months and closed the door behind him. I crept up the stairs and knocked on the door. He opened it just enough to peek out. "What?"

"I'm sorry… to bother you," I stuttered, "but this is the room I've been sleeping in." I felt the heat rising in my cheeks, my face turning beet red. When I finally got my composure, I said. "If you don't mind, I'll get some of my things out of the way so you have room for yours."

"Come back later," he said. "I'm going to change my clothes. I'll be out in two shakes of a lamb's tail. Then you can take what you want." He closed the door in my face.

I stood there embarrassed, my cheeks getting even hotter, this time because he was rude and I was angry for being treated that way.

After Charles was home a few days, I built this fantasy about him. I imagined when he came home from his stint in the army, he would see me as a woman, sweep me up in his arms and carry me off to a new and wonderful life, and we would live happily ever after. We'd have three or four kids and life would be good. Alas, it was only a dream and it didn't even come close to the truth. Now that Charles was home for the holidays, it turned into one of the nicest Christmas since coming to America.

His sister, Mary, came home from college the next day, and I dreaded it. Although she was friendly and nice, Mary was a slob, and I had to clean up after her all the time. She never lifted her finger to pick up anything. Her clothes were always thrown all over her bed and piled on every chair in the room. She'd put something on then discard it the next minute, and it would land in a heap on the floor. I had to go and pick them up, but the worst was most of the time I also had to wash and iron them again. That's life when you have to work for other people. Some day I would have a housekeeper or at least someone to come in and clean my home!"

It was difficult doing things for someone like Mary because she didn't appreciate anything and was spoiled. I was glad Mrs. Mack was grooming me to be a waitress at the Moline Café. The sooner, the better. I had to get away from this housework and meet people my own age. When I started as a waitress, I'd have more free time to go out with friends.

Sunday was my day off and I could use that time as I saw fit the whole day to myself. The worst of me working in the Moline Café were the high school kids who came in. They were carefree and had no sense also mean. I always wished I'd had it as easy. They treated me as their servant and were real messy, throwing things and spilling their drinks, making a big mess on the table. They usually ordered one banana split and five spoons and two cokes with extra straws. After I brought the straws, they'd open one end it and blow the paper off and it flew all over the floor. After they left I had to clean it all up.

To top it off they never thought to leave a tip. They made fun of my accent and were so mean they sometimes made me cry. I remember one bad day a rowdy bunch came in, and I asked someone else to wait on them because I was tired of being treated so badly. Our soda jerk named Charley came out from behind the counter and laid down the law to them. He said, if they didn't behave and treat me with respect, they'd be barred from the place. After that they were nicer to me and even left a tip once in awhile.

How sad. They had everything and didn't appreciate it. I wished I could go to school and have just a little of what they had. I would have liked to be carefree and not have a thought in my head except flirting, enjoying a coke with friends, going to the prom, having a boyfriend and just enjoying each day. Going to sleep at night without a worry in my head that's a life I haven't had in a long time.

Of course, the job had many drawbacks, especially for me because of the language barrier. Odd things always happened to me because of that.

One day I was stationed at the counter for the breakfast shift when an old man with rotten teeth and stringy gray hair sat on one of the stools and ordered "graveyard-stew." Not knowing what that was, I asked him to repeat it three times and he got so angry. He said, "You stupid girl, if you can't understand English you shouldn't be working here." "Graveyard Stew and bring it to me right now, or else."

Or else what, I thought, as I rushed to the kitchen.

It happened to be a very busy morning, and I didn't have time to fool around with a character like him. In the kitchen, I ordered gravy and stew. Mrs. Mack was preparing soup and heard my order.

She looked at me puzzled. "What did you order?" I repeated what I thought the man had said. "That can't be right, Maria," she said, "Stew is already in gravy. He must have ordered something else."

"No," I said, "I asked him a few times and he always said the same thing."

"Maybe so," she said "but I'd better go find out what he wants."

"No! Mrs. Mack, please don't go ask him. He's already mad and thinks I'm stupid. He called me stupid."

"I am sorry about that," she said, "but I have to find out what the man really wants."

By now the man was fuming and even snarled at her. "You better hire help that understands English if you want to keep your customers," he yelled.

She tried to pacify him. "I'm sorry, sir." If you just tell me what you ordered I'll fix it and bring it to you myself."

The two men sitting on either side of him spoke up loud, "Graveyard stew."

The old man cringed and looked around to see who heard, but the other people at the counter were busy eating and not paying attention. The old fool looked up and nodded. I followed Mrs. Mack into the kitchen to find out what he had ordered.

"It's simple Maria," she said, "grave-yard stew is milk toast."

"Milk toast? Then why in the world didn't he say that? Why would anyone call it graveyard stew?"

She laughed. "It's slang. Graveyard stew is for people who're sick or have no teeth." She showed me what to do and went out with me to serve him.

It must have been embarrassed because he kept his head down the whole time he was eating and left me a 25 cent tip. That was a lot for only milk toast and coffee in 1952.

Chapter 19

Two years went by like the wind and very little changed. I was working harder than ever, not only at the Mackenzie's but also the Café. My English was getting better every day. Monday was my day off from the Café, and I was going shopping for a dress, to wear at a new club opening Saturday night. They'd been advertising it for months. Arty Shaw and his band were to perform at the grand opening.

I was wearing a bright yellow blouse and tight fitting red jeans. What a beautiful day, I thought, as I stepped out the door and headed down town. Winter was finally behind us and the bright sun made me feel alive. I walked towards Main Street, almost dancing. I stopped at the Moline to pick up my meager paycheck. With what I made doing housework, and the few tips for bussing dishes, I'd finally saved enough to buy a new dress. Most of the earnings still went to my folks.

When I came out of the Café, I turned right on Main Street and walked towards down town. I was so intent in where I was going, I didn't notice what was happening behind me. My friend Gloria told me later when we met at the Hamburger Haven. "I saw you come out of the Moline," she said laughing. "I waved, but you didn't see me and kept going. I noticed two men coming from opposite directions, staring at you, so I watched for awhile, and when the men came to the corner, they collided! They'd been so intent watching you wiggling down the street, they didn't watch where they were going; it was really funny to see."She went on, "At first they were hollering at each other and then they saw the hilarity of it all and start laughing. When they parted they were shaking their heads, grinning from ear to ear. They turned once more and their eyes followed you until you were out of sight and then they went their spread way," she added. I had to giggle at the story it was hilarious and Gloria and I had a good laugh over it. I did find the perfect dress and it fit me like a clove. I could hardly wait for Saturday night. On Saturday my friend, Gloria Burdon and her boyfriend Jim Lewis were picking me up for the dance.

"You look great," Gloria said as I got into the car.

"Jim chimed in with a back handed compliment, "Maria, what did you do to yourself? You look different."

I was pleased that they both noticed because I'd taken special care with my make-up that evening. I knew I looked pretty and it felt good to hear it.

When we got to the dance, Arty Shaw and his band were playing "In the Mood" and the floor was crowded with jitter-buggers. Some were really into it, whirling, flipping and jiving to the music. It was fun watching them for awhile, but I wasn't going to stand on the sidelines for long. I had to be in the middle of things. Dancing was my passion, and no one could keep me off the dance floor. I quickly found a partner and to jitter-bugged with.

While I danced, Gloria and Jim found us a small table and ordered soft drinks. They didn't serve hard liquor there because it was against the law. But a cocktail lounge just across the road served the hard stuff for people old enough to drink. The next song was a slow ballad, and Gloria and Jim danced to it while I sat and watched, enjoying the music.

As the evening wore on it got so crowded there wasn't much room on the dance floor so we just stood swaying to the music and listening to Helen Morgan's great voice. Later, during intermission, we went outside for some fresh air and to cool off a bit. It was already getting a little rowdy out there. A bottle of booze was passed around, hidden in a paper bag, and they were spiking bottles of Seven-up with it.

Some guys must've been nipping it for awhile because they'd already too much to drink. Minutes later an argument started between two guys over a girl named Lisa. The guy who brought her was upset because she danced with the other guy who happened to be her ex-boyfriend. It didn't last long, typical of the dances we went to, always one or two fights and mostly over a girl. I didn't have a boyfriend yet and usually went to dances with my girlfriends, so I never had to worry that a fight would start over me. Going with Gloria and Jim and without my own date was great. I had my pick of guys and was free to dance with all of them.

While we were standing around outside, someone handed me a seven up and I took a big swig. I gagged and the fluid came gushing out of my mouth. Unfortunately, Jim was standing there and got sprayed. "This is the worst stuff I ever tasted," I said.

"Oh, come on, Maria," Jim replied, "don't be such a goody-goody. A little drink isn't going to hurt you. Here, take another swig and this time swallow it. Look what you did to my shirt. It's all wet and I smell like a brewery. What if the cops pick me up?"

"I don't drink," I said, it tastes awful. How can you guys drink that stuff?"

Jim took the bottle and another long, slow swig.

"Ah," he said, handing the bottle to a friend who took a big swig and handed it back to him.

"If you don't want the cops to smell booze on you, you better take it easy on that stuff. Remember you're the driver."

"So what? It's none of your damned business. Stop bugging me, Maria. You're not my girlfriend. If you don't like it, find another ride home."

Gloria stepped between us and tried to calm him with a kiss. She took a sip from the bottle, but he pushed her away, turned and started talking to his buddies. While he wasn't looking, Gloria emptied half the bottle out onto the ground. Then she refilled it with plain Seven-Up and gave it back. "Here," she said, "but take it easy, okay?"

He took another big swig. "Mum!"

"Come on," Gloria whispered to me, "let's go back inside. I have to go to the bathroom."

"So do I, let's get in line. It took almost an hour to get into the john.

When we came back, the music had already started and everyone was dancing. I didn't want Jim to be mad at me so I asked him to jitter-bug. "That is, if it's okay with Gloria?" I said.

"Sure," she said, "you two dance well together. Go show them what you got." Jim grumbled a bit but gave in.

Jim and I really fit well when dancing the jitter-bug. The band played, "I've Got a Girl in Kalamazoo," a Glenn Miller song and great to swing to. While we were dancing, the strap of my dress came undone and the strings were just flying loose. I could feel it, but we were going full speed, and I couldn't stop to tie it.

Jim was swinging me out and under and flipping me over his head, then pulling me through his legs. A lot of dancers stopped to watch us. We kept going, enjoying the attention. Everyone clapped when we finished, but I was worn out and ready to collapse. After we sat down, Gloria came over and tied my straps. "You know one reason they were all so excited?" She giggled. "The guys were hoping your other strap would come loose and your dress would slip down to your waist. I heard they made bets!"

"Well," I said, "They must been disappointed because the dress fits pretty tight. It wouldn't have fallen off."

We listened to the music for another hour or so. Gloria and Jim danced to "I'll Be Seeing You in all the Old Familiar Places." It was the last dance. It was great fun but it was 1:00 AM. And I was exhausted. I went right to bed when I got home. I was glad it was Sunday and I didn't have to work.

Maria, Gypsy Princess

The next time Gloria and I had dinner together she told me she and Jim had an argument on the way home from the dance. Gloria thought he drank too much and told him so. "He argued back," she said. "Maria, he blamed you for all of it. If you hadn't stuck your nose in our business, as he put it, I wouldn't have been mad at him. He said you had no right to tell him anything, and you are a busybody. Why couldn't we just go out alone sometimes?" he asked. "Let her get her own boyfriend to boss around."

She said the argument went on until they stopped at her front door. "All that, then he kissed me and said, 'Don't be mad. I love you.' Then he left. Men!"

"So what did you say?" I asked.

"I told him we had to talk because we've been arguing too much lately. We're meeting tomorrow for dinner and to talk," she added.

Gloria told me her folks always worried about her when she stayed out late. So they always left the porch light on until she got home.

"Ja," I said, "living with your parents is a drawback but also nice sometimes."

Gloria went on reliving the night after the dance. "The lights were on at the top of the stairs when I came in," she said. "My mother was still awake and called down to me, 'Is that you Gloria?'" "Yes ma." She giggled telling it, "Who do you think it is? Are you expecting someone else? I had a glass of milk and hit the hay."

Gloria didn't have to work Sunday either so she slept in. I asked how her morning was. "Well, ma, called up to me from the kitchen. 'Its ten o'clock, are you going to sleep all day?'" Gloria told me, she went down to breakfast and her mother grilled her about the dance. "Ma pleases not so early in the morning," Gloria said.

Her mother went on that it wasn't early. She had slept half the day away. "Then ma asked me if I had plans for today. I told her I was meeting you for an early movie, and then I'd meet Jim for supper." "My father came into kitchen so I was able to get away from my mother's questions." "But they're glad we're friends," Gloria said, "They really like you. They think you have a good head on her shoulders." Gloria's parents weren't too keen on Jim. They thought he drank too much.

I told her, "I think you're parents are great!"

"Yeah," Gloria said, "but my folks drive me crazy sometimes. They always want to know where I'm going and when I'll be back. Maria, you have it made," she said, you don't have to answer to anyone."

With a big sigh, I said, "Ja, its okay, but I wouldn't mind if someone worried and cared about me as much as your folks do. Not that my folks don't care. It's just they live so far away and can't be there for me like yours are. So be happy and enjoy it while you can."

"Sure, that's what you think, but I have to live it, and most of the time it's a bore".

Gloria and I were walking to the movie house, and I asked what her dreams were.

"Oh, not too big," she said. "I just want a good man, a house and a couple of kids. I'm very easy to please. How, about you?"

"I would like the same some day, but my dream has always been to be a dancer or even a film star. California is where I want to go, to get out of this God forsaken place, named North Dakota." Being Ginger Rogers would be nice. Now, she can really dance!" We kept on yakking all the way to the theater.

Chapter 20

Gloria and I became girlfriends early 1952 when I started working at the Moline Café. We hung out together and went to movies and enjoyed each other's company.

A few weeks later Gloria and Jim and I were going to another dance, and they were bringing a blind date for me, a friend of Jim's. When they picked me up, I was surprised that a man I didn't know was driving the car, a new white Studebaker. Gloria and Jim sat in the backseat, so I had to get in front next to the stranger.

Gloria and Jim spoke up at the same time. "This is P.J. Kruger. P.J., this is Maria Reule."

"Hi," we said at the same time too. I sat back and tried to enjoy the ride and make small talk with Gloria, but I wasn't comfortable. I didn't know why I felt uneasy, maybe because the guy was so much older and a smooth talker. He was dressed in a nice pair of slacks and a sport shirt; with dark hair, brown eyes and a straight nose. I guess you would say he was good looking in a rakish sort of way, but his smile seemed more like smirk, almost Satanic. Or was it my imagination? I couldn't tell.

He wanted me to sit closer to him. "Don't be shy," he said and grabbed my hand and tried to put me next to him. I withdrew my hand and moved as far away as I could. He gave me a sideways glance, and there was that smirk again. At the dance the boys went to get us some drinks, and we found a small table way in the back of the room. While they were gone, I asked Gloria if she knew him and how old he was.

"I think Jim said he was twenty-five, but I really don't know him."

Just then they came back and Jim asked Gloria to dance. P.J. sat next to me and slipped his arm around my back. I moved away, and he pretended not to notice, babbling away while I scrutinized him. I was right, he was a lot older. Twenty-five was much too old for me.

I always had fun at dances because I loved to dance, so I had fun in spite of
P.J. and his subtle advances. He held me too tight when we were danced, and I tried to push him away to discourage him. But he was strong and kept pulling me back in a tight embrace.

From time to time between dancing Jim and P. J. went to the bar that was separated from the dance area. When they came back they were feeling no pain. We danced for hours and much later when P.J. and I came back to the table after a dance, Gloria and Jim were nowhere to be seen. I asked P.J. if he knew where they went. He just shook his head. "Come on, let's go and find them. I'm sure they're just outside having a drink. It was almost time to go home, so we went outside and we searched everywhere and asked many people if they'd seen them. Finally a guy told us they had taken off with some other friends.

I was very upset. How could they leave me here with a total stranger? Angry tears filled my eyes. How could my best friend betray me so?

"Its okay," P.J. said, "I'll take you home."

"But I don't know you," I said, "I'd rather not go with you alone in your car."

"Oh, I promise I won't bite. I'm really nice when you get to know me."

"I'd rather go home with someone else," I said.

"Well, I doubt you'll find someone this late date." He glanced around the almost empty parking lot. "There aren't many people left, but you can ask around and see if you can find someone going your direction. I'll wait right here in the car until you come back, okay?"

I frantically rushed around knocking on car windows, asking people, but none were going my way, or they didn't want to be bothered. I had no recourse but to go with P.J. I didn't like it, but it was too far out of town, and I really didn't have another way to get home. I only had a dollar to my name.

When we were almost back to town, P. J. asked if I would like to go up spoon hill and watch the lights. I told him no, but he acted like he didn't hear me and drove up the hill anyway. I kept telling him to take me home, but he just ignored me and kept driving. I told him to stop the car and let me out. I'd walk home. But he kept driving all the way up.

"Now, isn't this a beautiful view?"

I did agree it was, but still wanted to go home. I was tired and wanted my bed and told him so. I was sitting way over close to the window, and I tried to open the door but it was locked, and I was so flustered I couldn't pull up the button. I hollered at him to unlock it so I could get out. With one hand held the button down and grabbed my arm and pulled so hard I thought he'd pull it off. He moved closer to me, "How about a kiss first, he said then I'll take you home."

I turned to just give him a peck, but he wasn't satisfied. He reached across me, pulled a lever and the seat flopped back, and I screamed as I fell backwards. Before I knew what was happening he was on top of me pulling on my clothes. I fought him with teeth and nails, kicking and scratching. I drew blood, I think, and he got angry and held me even tighter.

I screamed, "Get off me!" But he was too strong. I started to cry. "Please, let me go." I pounded on his chest. He had his mouth on mine, and I bit his lip. I kept trying to kick him, but I was pinned down. He held my hands over my head with one hand, pulling my pants down with the other. I still can't figure out how fast he had his pants down. There was a fierce stabbing pain between my legs.

I screamed, "You pig, you're hurting me!"

He just kept holding my hands above my head in a steel grip, pounding into me and making awful noises, sounding like the pig he was. He was breathing hard and his breath smelled of booze. He didn't care if he hurt me. All he cared about was satisfying him self. I didn't know anything could be so horrible. All my dreams of happily-ever-after with a loving man and children seemed gone forever.

It was a violation of my body. I had no idea sex could be so fierce. I was biting my own lips now, trying to keep from crying. I was angry. I should have stopped him somehow. But he was too strong, I couldn't move. Finally his body shook and he finished. He had the sadistic smile I witnessed in the car and at the dance. He had planned it, and I was sure Jim set it up. He tried to kiss me, and I slapped him and pushed him away. I will not cry, I thought, I won't give him the satisfaction.

"Take me home now, you dirty swine." I tried to open the door to get out, but it was still locked. I should've walked home as soon as we got here.

He just kept grinning and moved back to his side. I tried to pull up my pants, but it was hard lying flat with the dammed seat still down. I was so ashamed. "Put the seat up," I mumbled.

He reached over me, pulled the lever, and the seat jumped forward so fast I almost hit my head on the dashboard. I was lucky not to knock my teeth out. I pulled my pants up and adjusted my clothing, and that's when I felt the sticky oozing between my legs, and it made my sick to my stomach.

"Let me out of this dammed car, you pig," I yelled. "I'll walk home."

"Oh, come on, Maria, don't be like that," he said. "I like you. I'll gladly take you out again so we can get to know each other better."

"I know enough about you, and I hope you drop dead. Now, let's go."

Maria Reule Woelfl

I moved as far away from him as I could, and we drove home, not speaking a word. As soon as the car stopped in front of the house, I jumped out and slammed the door behind me. I ran to the front door, my hand shaking so badly I fumbled to find my key. When I finally got the door open, I quietly crept up the back stairs to the bathroom to clean myself up. I put a little water in the bottom of the tub, took off my dress and panties and sat in the tub, shaking. "Mama," I cried, "where are you? I need you, Mama. I have no one to talk to." Oh, how I wished my sister Vickie was here. She would know what to do. She would hold me and comfort me. Oh God, why were all my sisters so far away?

I was in shock, and there was blood in the water. I don't remember how long I sat there, but when the water turned cold it brought me back to awareness. I still sat for awhile, confused about what to do next. I finally got out, dried myself off, and crept downstairs. I took my clothes off and threw them down in the basement. I put on a nightgown and slipped into bed. My last thought was of my father. If he knew he would thrash me with his cane. Then I thought no Papa wouldn't hurt me he would comfort me instead. But he would knock P. J. teeth's out. Papa, I'm sorry I let you down. I should have gotten away.

I didn't dare tell anyone or go to the police. I doubt they would have believed me, and I was scared I would be sent back to Europe. In those days men got away with anything and it would have been my fault.

I awoke to chimes as the clock struck 9:00. Oh, I thought, I over slept. Then it dawned on me it was Sunday and I didn't have to go to work. I still lived with the Mackenzie's, but now I slept in the den down stairs because the room I had before was used by Mrs. Mack's sister, Grace, who was visiting for awhile. She was planning to move here permanently in a couple of months. So I had to find other dwellings. When I went into the kitchen, the family had already eaten breakfast, and Grace was washing the dishes. I started to fix some toast, but Grace said there was still some pancake batter left and I could make myself some if I wanted. I thanked her and said I would finish the dishes after I ate breakfast.

She said okay and turned toward me. "You look kind of peaked. Is something wrong?"

"Oh, I didn't sleep too well last night I guess, I'm still tired."

"Ja, you probably stayed out too late dancing."

"You're right. I'm sure I'll feel better after a good night's sleep."

You might wonder why Grace would say ja, there where many Germans people lived in North Dakota and most of them said ja instead of yes. Grace left the kitchen, and I was left with my thoughts, that I wanted to forget. It never happened, I thought, but one can't wish rape away. It was deeply embedded in me and would be there the rest of my life. I knew I would never forget what happened. How could I? My life was ruined now. The thought of being with one man and living happily-ever-after was gone. I had been used in the most vile way. Since I had no one to talk to I'd have to live with the guilt and shame from now on. I had to put it out off my mind, but how?

I had gone all through World War II fleeing and being scared of the Russians soldiers, afraid my sisters or I would be raped by them, but, no, I had to come all the way to America, the land of the free and the brave, to be raped. He used me and couldn't care less how much he hurt me. Begging didn't stop him and he didn't consider my feelings at all. My self-esteem and self-respect were at low ebb now. I felt used, and my feelings toward sex distorted.

Much later when I started to date, I never knew if a man meant it when he said he loved me or if he just wanted to use me for sex. It took me the longest time to trust any man.

That week I walked around in a daze. Even Mrs. Mack noticed something was wrong. I was depressed and weepy, and had no idea what to do next. Mrs. Mack asked what was wrong and why I was so down, and I told her I was just tired, that I had stayed out too late the other night and hadn't caught up on my sleep yet.

"You don't look right to me," she said. "Are you sure you're not coming down with something?"

"I don't think so, but I'll take it easy the next few days, okay."

She seemed satisfied with my answer, but on her way out she asked what I was going to do my day off.

"Oh, Gloria and I are going to a movie and a get bite to eat."

"Good, I'll see you later."

When I saw Gloria I tore into her. "Why did you leave me there with that beast, P.J.?"

"Why, what happened?" she asked.

"He forced himself on me. You stranded me at the dance, and he, he… raped me."

"Oh, my God Maria! I'm so sorry." She put her arms around me, but I pulled away, too angry for comfort. She crabbed my hand and pulled me to a bench to talk

"I'm angrier with Jim," I said after we sat down. "I'm sure P.J. made a deal for Jim to leave me there with him. They set it up, and you left me there with that animal from hell!"

"Oh, Maria, Jim wouldn't do such a thing. Not on purpose."

"Yes, he would. He hates me and doesn't want us to stay friends. He was jealous because you and I are close friends and spend so much time together."

"Oh, I doubt he's smart enough to think that way."

"You might be surprised what jealousy can do to people. Anyway, it's too late now. The damage is done and nothing can change it."

"I am sorry. I had no idea what kind of guy he was. I only met P.J. that night. Please let me help, Maria. Talk to me. Tell me what I can do. Oh, wait till I see Jim... Oh my God, if he did set it up..."

I put my hand on her arm. "No, I don't want you to tell Jim anything, I said. Promise you won't. I know he'd spread it around. It would be all over town in no time."

She saw the fear in my eyes. "All right, she said, but won't you talk to me about it? It would probably help."

"No. I just want to forget the whole thing. I'm trying to put the whole episode behind me, that is, if I can. And I don't ever want to hear his name again. Ever."

I forgave Gloria, but told her I'd never forgive Jim. I was sure he had fixed me up with that creep.

In the next weeks I kept myself busy. I couldn't stay home thinking. At the restaurant I met a few new people, and before long I started seeing a nice boy named Mark, and we just had good clean fun. One Saturday night Mark and I went with another couple to the dance, and when we picked them up the girl, Marsha by name, acted very strange when we were introduced. She looked at me with hate in her eyes, then turned and put her arms around Mark. She tried to give him a big kiss, but he turned his head. I must have grinned because she stuck her tongue out at me and walked around the car in a huff.

At the dance, Marsha tried to sit next to Mark, but I was too fast and pulled him next to me at the table. She had to sit on the other side with her boyfriend, Harry, and again she gave me that look. I wondered what her problem was. Why is she being so rude? I thought. Later I found out she and Mark used to go steady, and she felt he was still her property. He had moved on, but she hadn't let go of him yet. She was just going out with Harry to make Mark jealous, but Mark couldn't care less. We ordered drinks, and Mark and I went to dance, Marsha gave me another look that could kill. When we came back she wanted to dance with Mark, but he told her, "Ask Harry. I'm sure he'd love to dance with you."

She was in a huff when she pulled Harry onto the dance floor. Mark and I sipped our drinks, ordered cheeseburgers, and enjoyed watching the dancers. When they came back, Harry ordered some food for them, and

Maria, Gypsy Princess

everything seemed okay. I leaned my head on Mark's shoulder and hummed along with the tune for awhile.

Suddenly Marsha kicked me in the shin really hard, and without thinking I hauled off and slapped her across the face.

"You bitch!" She rubbed her cheek and started to howl.

Mark and Harry thought I had gone crazy. When I told them, they didn't believe she started it. They blamed me and were angry.

Later when the guys weren't looking, she had a big smirk, and stuck her tongue out at me again. The guys didn't see any of it. She thought she had won that round by making me the heavy. We ate silently without looking at each other. When I finished, I tried to stand up to go to the bathroom, but my leg buckled and I grimaced with the pain. I looked down and it was all swollen and black and blue.

"What's the matter with you now?" Mark said. But when he saw my leg, with the skin broken and blood was oozing out; he realized I had told them the truth. She did kick me.

Mark and Harry apologized, but Marsha didn't say a word. She just sat there pouting. Mark and I danced a couple of slow dances, and then went home. It was too bad Harry was stuck with Marsha. Harry was real nice and a friend of Mark's and Mark felt badly that Marsha was treating him so shabbily. Mark and I only dated for a short while. There was no spark, so we drifted apart.

Life went on as usual, hard work and very little fun and not much money.

After the incident with P.J., I managed as best as I could. I even met a really nice young man, a sailor by the name of Marvin Holstein. Marvin was on leave from the Navy, visiting his father in Jamestown. He lived with his mother in Bemidji Minnesota, and would only be in town for two weeks before he had to report back to his ship, which was docked in Boston.

We hit it off great and saw each other every day. The last day before he had to go back, we went to a movie and stopped for a hamburger and a coke afterward. Then we went to the park and held hands and walked around, talking and getting to know each other better.

We brought a small blanket and laid it on the grass under a tree. We smooched and rolled around for awhile. It got a little hot and heavy and we felt each other up a little too, and Marvin put his penis close to me and rubbed it between my legs and held it there. If he went inside it was only a little. Mostly we just held each other close. We both had tears in our eyes but didn't go any further. We stayed that way for quite awhile, just kissing and talking and feeling sad. After an hour or so he took me home, and we said good night and had a last kiss on the doorstep. He promised to write and I did the same, and I felt better than I had in a long time.

In a couple of weeks I got a letter from him saying how he enjoyed meeting me and hoped I was well but that he wouldn't have much time to write because they were getting the ship ready to get on the way. They didn't know when because it was all hush-hush and in the meantime they kept them all hopping. He would write again as soon when he had time.

I didn't answer right away because I didn't write English yet and had to find someone to help me. Since the incident with P.J., Gloria and I weren't close any more. She was still going out with Jim. I knew I'd find someone to help me with the letter. But a week went by and I hadn't written to Marvin yet.

One day when we were in the kitchen drying the dishes, out of the blue Mrs. Mack asked, "Maria are you gaining weight? You look much heavier to me."

"I don't know," I said, "maybe a few pounds. My clothes are getting a little tight around the middle. I haven't weighed myself lately."

She looked at me closer and turned me around. "When is the last time you had your period?"

"I don't know. It's been awhile. I haven't paid much attention. Why?"

"Well, it looks to me like you're pregnant. Who have you been with lately?"

"No one," I said, almost dropping the plate I was drying. "The last person I went out with was Marvin, but we didn't really do anything."

"Well, something must've happened because you look pregnant to me."

I stared at her. "I can't be pregnant, Mrs. Mack. I just can't. What would I tell my folks?"

The idea horrified me. I could not tell Vati. He would be so disappointed in me. My mind was in turmoil. Pregnant! I thought. If it was true, I'd have to give the baby away. That's it. I'd give it away.

I turned back to Mrs. Mack. "How can you be so sure?"

She smiled. "I've been around long enough to tell when someone is with child."

I sank into a chair by the kitchen table. "Oh, Mrs. Mack, I don't know what to do. Please help me."

"First we have to make sure. I know a doctor, a friend. He'll examine you without asking too many questions. I'll make an appointment tomorrow."

The doctor indeed confirmed my worst fear. I was pregnant.

A few days later, Mrs. Mack asked if I wanted to write to Marvin and let him know he'd be a father soon. I wasn't sure. So she said, "If you don't want to tell him you have to make up your mind, either keep the baby or give it

Maria, Gypsy Princess

away. If that's what you want, I can arrange for you to go to a home for unwed mothers in Fargo. I can take you next week. You have to decide soon because you won't be able to hide it much longer." She gave me a hug. "You think on it, honey, and let me know your decision in the next few days. I'll have to make all the arrangements, so let me know real soon, okay?"

I nodded, but I felt dazed, and my mind wasn't working.

The fallowing week was hectic and I didn't know if I was coming or going. I couldn't make up my mind. I knew one thing for sure. I didn't want my parents to know I was pregnant. They lived in Driscoll now, and it was better they didn't know. If I was going to give the baby away, they didn't ever have to know at all.

Before Mrs. Mack asked me if I was pregnant I really didn't comprehend it all or even realizing I was pregnant. I only knew something was wrong because I had these cravings. I could not get enough grapes or cherries, and they are still my favorite fruit to this day. It was in a dilemma, but I finally decided to go to Fargo to the home for unwed mothers to give the baby away. I could always change my mind later on and keep it.

It never occur to me that I got pregnant the night P.J. forced himself on me. Maybe my mind couldn't or wouldn't believe it. I must have been in denial. To me, P.J. Kruger no longer existed.

Mrs. Mack came through for me and made all the arrangements at St Agnes Home for unwed mothers. When we arrived there, we were hustled right in and a very efficient looking lady took us into a room and told us to be seated, that she would get the director to interview us right away.

About twenty minutes later a tall, severe looking woman walked into the room and introduced herself as Miss Hathaway. She sat behind the desk and shuffled some papers around, not saying a word, and that made me nervous. When she finally looked up, I must've looked frightened because she looked right at me and said, "Don't be afraid of me. I really don't bite. Now, I just have a few questions to ask to make sure you understand what is expected of you here. We want to make absolutely sure you want to give your baby away, also do you understand that's why you're here?" You'll have room and board until the day you give birth. After that you have to make other arrangements where you'll live. While you're here you'll have to abide by the rules of the house." She then took a piece a paper from her desk and handed it to me. "Here is a sheet with the rules and regulations on it, if you don't understand some of them Rachel, my assistant will explain later. For now, I'll show you to your room, and while you get settled in, I'll have a little talk with Mrs. Mackenzie."

As we walked she droned on. "Later you will be examined by a doctor to find out how far along you are in your pregnancy then we'll know how long you'll be with us." She stopped so suddenly I almost ran into her. She turned and showed me to my assigned room. "You'll be sharing with a girl named Joan. You'll meet her later at meal time.

"By the way," she went on, "the girls only go by first names here. Only the doctor and I know last names. So please don't ask the other girls their full names unless they volunteer it. Their personal information is their own business so don't ask too many questions," alright.

All I could do was nod. She showed me my bed and the drawer I was to use. Mrs. Mack came and gave me a big hug and said she would be in touch with me, and if I needed anything to let Miss Hathaway know, and she'd do whatever she could to help. I met all the other girls at lunchtime. There were seven of them. I was number eight. We were introduced and had a cold lunch of sandwiches and fruit, and it was very good. After we finished we were to go rest in the play room until the doctor arrived.

I was the first one to be called into see doctor Handle, a short, chubby man with little glasses he looked over when he talked. He was nice and efficient with a friendly smile. He asked me questions about my pregnancy, how far along I was. I told him I really didn't know, but I thought four or five months.

"Hmm, well, we'll just have to check you out and see. What did your other doctor tell you?"

"Oh, he said five months."

"Hmm, okay, we shall see what's going on inside you and how the baby is faring.

He rang for his nurse and she came in and helped me up on an examining table. Then she stood by and assisted him, handing him the instruments he needed to look inside. It was very uncomfortable. This was only the second time been to a doctor since we came to this country. I was ashamed to have a man look at my vagina, even if he was a doctor. I didn't want him to poke his finger into me, so I clamped my legs shut and the nurse had to pry them open. "Now open wide so the doctor can examine you."

He was all business like. After he finished his examination, he told me everything looked really good and the baby was in the right position. "I'll see you next month, okay?" And I was dismissed.

I went down to the room, and three girls were lying on a mattress on the floor there for us to lie around on. They had covered it with a sheet and set some pillows on it. The carpet looked cheap, also the sofa and two chairs. It was all nice and clean and the girls all took their shoes off when they came into the room, which is why it stayed so clean. There were magazines on a small coffee table. I picked one up to look at it, thinking there were pictures inside but, alas, they were all true love or true romance stories. Not

Maria, Gypsy Princess

appropriate reading material under the circumstances, I thought. With us all being pregnant, we should read how to stay away from boys and abstain from sex, not true romance stories. We should read the Bible, but it was hidden on a corner table out of the way. After awhile I enjoyed reading the magazines too, although I didn't understand much because my English wasn't that good and neither was my reading.

I read the list of dos and don'ts and I didn't like most of the rules, but I could live with them. The one I really disliked was we were not allowed to go outside at all, and I felt like I was in prison. We had the same routine every day and it got trying. I wanted to go outside, walk in the park, take off my shoes and run bare foot through the grass. The only thing I was allowed to do was walk out on a small balcony in the behind the house, where all you could see was the back of other buildings and a dirty little alley. Steps lead down to the street from the balcony so I could've escaped if I wanted to. Just to be free for a few hours, but where would I go? I was a prisoner of my own making so I had to endure.

I was only there a month and half when I decided I couldn't stand it another day, so I asked Miss Hathaway to please call Mrs. Mack so I could talk to her. I had to get out of there. I hoped Mrs. Mack would write a letter for me. I decided to tell Marvin after all that I was pregnant and he was the father. At that time I really didn't know if he was the father or not. Mrs. Mack was skeptical about the whole thing, meaning me writing to Marvin, but she did as I asked.

You might question the sanity of it all. Why didn't I know that Marvin couldn't be the father? I think it was part denial, part naiveté and mostly ignorance.

While waiting for Marvin's answer to my letter, Mrs. Mack found me a job with a nice couple in Moorhead Minnesota, a town just across the river from Fargo. They had two little girls, and went to work taking care of them. The mother and father worked for Hotel Moorhead.

I didn't hear from Marvin for quite awhile, and I thought he either didn't get the letter or just didn't care and threw it away. He must have thought, the heck with her, how do I know I am really the father? Not hearing from him made me sad, but I decided to keep the baby anyway.

In the meantime I did my work and stayed out of trouble. Since I was seven months pregnant I couldn't do otherwise. The couple I worked for lived in a basement and had two little girls. The apartment and their landlords, Melanie and Bruce Werner, lived up stairs. They also had two little girls, Lorie and Kim, so sometimes I would baby sit for them too. My bosses the Frymarks were wonderful people.

Maria Reule Woelfl

The basement apartment only had two bedrooms so I had to share the girls' room, and it was really crowded. One day I wanted to show off my culinary prowess by cooking stuffed cabbage for the family. I had watched my sisters make it when I was young and it always tasted great. But I made a booboo and I forgot to precook the rice before I mixed it into the meat, so after cooking the stuffed cabbage for over an hour the rice was still half raw and it tasted awful. The dinner was a disaster so we had to throw it out and we laughed about the mess I made later on.

I only worked for the Frymarks about a month before they started having marital problems. John, the husband, wanted out of the marriage. He was in love with his secretary and didn't want to be married to his wife, Anne, anymore. He was dark and handsome and sharp dressed, always immaculate, and hardly ever at home. In a word he was a womanizer. I felt sorry for Anne. She was a lost soul, distressed over the break up. Now they didn't need me to take care of the kids any more and had let me go. Anne took the girls and went to live with her parents until she figured out what she wanted to do next. So again I was out of a job with nowhere to go. Melanie took pity on me and said I could stay with them upstairs for the time being.

A week or so later a letter came from Marvin. He was sorry it took so long, but they were out on maneuvers and he couldn't write. He had talked to his chaplain who told him if he was sure the baby was his he should do the right thing and marry me. If not, he was to write and tell me so. Also he should ask if I wanted to marry him before making the commitment and to be absolutely certain he wanted to do this. "Maybe she doesn't even want to get married," the chaplain said.

I didn't know what to do. I was lonely and missed my family. I wished I could write to them and tell them the truth about the baby, but I was afraid Vati would be so disappointed in me. I had been telling them lies for months now and making excuses why I couldn't come for a visit. I longed for my father's arms and his stubbly beard. It is terrible to be all alone in a strange city, and now going even farther away to meet someone I hardly knew. I was terrifying. What if he didn't really want me? I'd be stranded in Boston.

I'd been through so many things in my life time. I guess I was used to disappointments by now.

After a few days weighing the pros and the cons of the situation, I asked Melanie if she would please write the letter for me. "Tell him, I accept his proposal of marriage and for him to make arrangements for me to come to Boston."

I was almost eight months pregnant now and as big as a house. I needed new clothes I couldn't afford, so I asked Marvin to wire some money for the train trip and little extra for expenses. A hundred and fifty dollars came

Maria, Gypsy Princess

by mail a few days later. I was also scared to death to take such a trip all by myself. After all, what did I know about this person? He was almost a total stranger to me. But it seemed I had to give it a try and see what the outcome would be.

The train ride was very uncomfortable and difficult for me. After all, I was eight months pregnant and it was a long way from home. While en route I had time to think about my family. I missed them more and more every mile that took me further away, especially my father and what would my sisters say if they knew of my condition. They were so far away I felt I no longer had any sisters.

I was too uncomfortable to sleep much, so I cried most of the way there. When I finally arrived in Boston I still had a ways to go to get to my destination. Marvin had rented us a small apartment not far from the wharf. He wanted to be close in case they had to ship out in a moment's notice. The cabby and I had a hard time understanding each other me with my foreign accent and he with his Boston one it was quiet some thing. I finally gave him the letter with the instructions, and a hour later we got to the right place.

The room was a walk up in an old building, and there were other tenants in the lower part. It was difficult to lug my stuff up the stairs in my condition so I ran outside and asked the cabby to carry in up for me. I waddled up the stairs into a strange place I was all alone and frighten. In Marvin letter he said he would be home, around six to seven that evening. It was three in the afternoon now so I had time on my hands.

It was a small place with a tiny bedroom and a tiny kitchen. The living area had a lumpy sofa and small round table with two chairs. The bathroom had a free standing tub, a toilet and not much more. I put my stuff away and took a hot bath, then stretched out on the bed for awhile. I must have dozed off because it was almost five when I awoke.

I got up, splashed some water on my face, combed my hair and put on my best smock, and looked to see what there was in the fridge to eat, not much. Well, I'd have to go shopping before Marvin arrived, otherwise we wouldn't have anything for our dinner. I went downstairs and knocked on a door. An old lady answered and asked who I was and what I wanted. I told her I had just moved in upstairs and wondered if a store was close by. I wanted to go buy some things for dinner. She took me outside, walked to the corner with me and pointed, "The store's just down the street, and you can see it from here."

I thanked her and waddled down to a deli, and to my good fortune they had all kinds of goodies. My dilemma was I didn't know what Marvin liked. I decided to take a little of everything, coleslaw, ham, turkey, roast beef and pickles also potato salad. When I came home, I put the stuff on plates and the rest in the fridge and set the table.

I sprayed on some perfume and sat down with a book to wait for my husband to be, to come home. I tried to read but couldn't concentrate. I didn't know what to expect from Marvin. It had been five months since we had seen each other and we'd spent only a little over a week together. I really didn't know much about him and of course he didn't know me either. I was getting panicky. What if he didn't like me after all? All these thoughts were whirling through my mind. What if he didn't want me? What would I do then?

Marvin arrived around seven and it was a quite a moment for both of us. After all, it's been awhile and I was slim and trim then. Now I was as large as a house. I was sure when Marvin saw me he would want to turn around and run back to the ship. When he came in he gave me a little kiss on the cheek and I hugged him and asked if he was hungry.

"Oh, I guess so, he said, but I'm afraid there isn't much in the ice box.

"Well, I said, "Let's open it and see." I opened the door and he was surprised when he saw all the goodies I had bought. I even bought a bottle of wine and two cupcakes for dessert.

"Come, let's sit and have a glass of wine and talk a little. Tell me about your ship. When are they planning to ship out?"

"I really can't tell you much," he said. 'They don't want us to know when we're going. It's all hush, hush."

"Oh, well, then I'll tell you what I've been doing and about my train trip here." He sat and I poured us each a glass of wine. We talked a little, but the whole situation was awkward for both of us.

I asked how long he could stay, and he told me he had to leave Sunday noon to be report for duty that evening. It was Friday now, so we only had tomorrow to be with each other. That didn't give us enough time to get reacquainted. We just had made do with the time we had. I poured him another glass of wine, hoping it would relax him a little. He seemed very nervous. He kept turning his glass around and around looking into it like he wanted to find an answer in the liquid.

I put the food on the table and said, "Let's eat." We sat and ate without saying a word for about ten minutes. Finally I couldn't stand it any longer. "Pennies for your deep thoughts?" I said.

He looked up from his plate with a dazed look I don't think he even knew where he was for a second. His eyes were like a deer startled by a car's headlights. I worried that there was something wrong with him. When he came to his senses he said.

"Oh, I was just thinking of my mother. She isn't happy with our situation. Not at all. Not at all."

"I suppose it must've been a great shock," I said. "Getting married to someone she doesn't know. Have you told her yet?"

"Yes, I wrote to her the same day I wrote you."

"What did she say?"

"She wasn't unhappy about it. She sent me a telegram asking me to be very sure I knew what I was doing."

"I guess she's right," I said. "It is a big step to take. I haven't told my parents yet. I don't know what they'll say when they find out, especially my father. I think he'll go through the roof. I'll have to send them a telegram to let them know where I am and all. When do you think we can go and get our marriage license?"

"I don't know exactly," he said, "I won't be able to get leave again for at least a week."

"Oh, you mean I have to sit around here alone for over a week?"

"Nothing I can do about that. That's the navy. You have to wait for everything." Let's not think about it right now. I'm sure you must be very tired after your long train ride."

"Yes, I am sort of and the baby is kicking a lot. He or she is probably tired too. Here feel my belly. It's kicking up a storm right now."

He put his hand on my stomach and smiled. "Wow, a strong one. It kicks like it wants to get out right now. Does that hurt?"

"Well, it's a little annoying especially when I'm trying to sleep. He or she is supposed to be asleep at the same time, but it doesn't work out that way."

Marvin helped me put everything away and we got ready for bed. I used the bathroom first and crawled into bed. I almost fell asleep waiting for him to come. He must've been stalling, hoping I was asleep before he came to bed. I had my face to the wall and he eased himself into the bed not to wake me. We both lay very still, neither of us wanted to make the first move or touch. The silence was deafening.

I finally turned and put my arm around him, and he turned too. He gave me a kiss and that led to more, but it was awkward with my huge belly. He didn't quite know how to go about it, so it took some time and effort, poor fellow. He was a novice, just like me. Neither of us knew what to do. He finally got so frustrated he gave up, and I was just as happy he did. I was too tired and needed a little fore play or something. It just didn't seem to work like it was supposed to.

Of course, I really didn't know how it was supposed to work. All I knew was what I saw in the movies, all so romantic and this was not it. I was in extreme discomfort, and I am sure he was too because he gave up and said, "We're both tired tonight. We'll try again tomorrow."

I said okay and we kissed and tried to go to sleep but it took me quite awhile. Marvin was breathing evenly so I knew he went right to sleep. I didn't want to admit it, but I was a little disappointed in our first encounter and hoped it would get better or else this marriage wouldn't work.

The next morning I was tired so I slept in. Marvin got up and made his own breakfast and left, not waiting for me to get up. I got up, took a quick bath and had a bite to eat. Then waited for him to return. When he came back he said he went for a walk and asked if I wanted go out and look around a little bit, find a place to have lunch then go to a movie. I said okay. We would ask one of our neighbors if there was a Café close by. I put my clothes on and we left. We walked to the restaurant and had a great lunch. Then we found a movie not far from our apartment. I picked a musical. Marvin wasn't too keen about it, but he liked westerns so "Anne Get Your Gun" seemed close to both our liking.

I enjoyed the movie very much, but again it was awkward afterward. It seemed we didn't have much in common. We went walking in the park and he talked a little about his family and I talked about mine. I could tell he wanted to tell me something else but he kept it to himself.

I figured he'd open up after awhile and let me know what was sitting so heavy on his heart and mind. When we went back to the apartment it got really quiet because we didn't know what to do with each other or what to say. Luckily, Marvin had brought a small radio along so he turned it on and listened to some music, and he asked me to dance and it was great to sway to the music again. It seemed I hadn't danced for ages. We danced for awhile and as we danced we got a little closer, and he started to kiss me so we sat on the sofa and smooched for awhile. When we parted he was breathing heavily and I could tell he wanted me.

He must have been thinking of last night because he straightened up, looked at his watch and asked me if I was getting hungry. I didn't realize how late it was getting so I said, "Ja, I'm always hungry now that I'm eating for two. The baby is constantly asking me to feed it. There's some wine left. Let's have some while I fix us something. Or would you rather do it yourself?"

"Oh no, I'll just come into the kitchen and keep you company. Whatever you fix is okay with me."

"Okay how about the kitchen sink?"

He grinned. "I get that in the navy every day and I have to like it or starve."

"Well, we don't want you starve. I'll take care of you. You'll like my omelet."

Maria, Gypsy Princess

I took a sip of my wine and he stood and nuzzled my neck and I felt good. Maybe it will work out after all, I thought. It was just too strange the first night. After all, we hadn't seen each other for so long. I started humming a German tune and he asked me about it and I tried to translate it as best I could, but it came out all jumbled up and we both laughed. So the ice was broken and we enjoyed our omelet and he complimented me on a job well done.

We put everything away, and I told him I'd have plenty of time tomorrow to clean up so we left the dishes in the sink and went back to the other room. A great dance number was playing on the radio so we danced some more, then finished the wine and went to bed.

This time it was easier, and he figured out how to work around my belly because we actually had sex, and it wasn't too bad. Since I hadn't anything to compare it with, I guess it was a five on the Richter scale.

My first time was such a violent and brutal act. Now with my big belly, I still didn't know what it should feel like. I didn't know if I'd ever feel comfortable having sex or know the difference between intercourse and love making. To me it seemed something your partner wants from you and you comply, but as far as I was concerned they could have it. It was too messy.

Maybe some day I'd be in love and enjoy making love with my man. He'd love me in return, and it would be great. That was yet to come. It might be Marvin, but it was too soon to tell.

When I awoke I was alone in the apartment. It was already 10:00. I was just starting to make myself something to eat when Marvin came back with some sweet rolls and we had breakfast together. Later he went out for a walk and brought back a newspaper so we sat on the sofa, and I looked at the funnies while he read the sports page.

He told me he found a Chinese café close by and we could go there later and get some takeout. So I took a bath and got dressed while he read the paper. He told me he had talked to the old lady downstairs and that he would call her to let me know when he'd be back.

"I hope I won't be gone more than a week," he said, "but I'll let you know, and when I get back we can go get out wedding license." He called his ship and found out he didn't have to report until the next morning so we'd have a few more hours together.

We went to the Chinese café later and decided to have dinner there and it was great fun. Our fortune cookies were in our favor and we laughed and were in great spirits. He walked me back to the apartment and I kissed him good bye and thought, What will I do for a week in a strange place not knowing anyone and very little money to my name?

Maria Reule Woelfl

Time went slowly. I met the lady downstairs. She had two children, a girl about five and a boy two years younger. She was very kind and felt sorry for me and my plight. I offered to baby sit if she needed to go out to the store. She thanked me and said she'd let me know if she needed me in the future. She wasn't married, and the father of her son was a married man and only came to see her once in awhile. She told me he was Catholic and didn't believe in divorce. Her daughter came from a previous marriage that didn't last very long.

She was Italian, older, about forty, with a dark complexion with raven hair, and she was really thin. She had her kids late in life and was madly in love with the man she was going with. He had money, so he took good care of her and the kids. If that's the life she wanted who was I to say nay or question her choices? My own life was a holy mess, and I didn't know where I would end up or how it would turn out.

Marvin was an easy-going guy, you might even call him sweet. That is, if you can call a man sweet? I think he was a bit of a mama's boy because he doted on her. Maybe it was just his kind heart showing? His parents divorced when he was very young and his mother hadn't remarried. So I guess he had to be the man of the house at an early age. I think that's why he was so thoughtful towards women. He was good husband material and I was lucky to have him. So I thought.

I didn't hear from Marvin for five days. Then he finally left a message with Helen, the lady downstairs. He told her he couldn't call sooner because he was on duty and couldn't get off the ship. He would call again Saturday at one o'clock and would I be downstairs so he could talk to me himself? Helen told him it was okay for him to call me there. So until Saturday I was alone waiting for his call.

When he called he said he would get a few days off starting Tuesday and that's when we could go get the marriage license. Tuesday came and we went to the courthouse and applied for a license. That's when we found out I couldn't get married without my parents' okay because I wasn't eighteen yet. So I had to write to my folks and ask for permission. The court gave us a legal document for them to fill out, and I sent it to Vati and Mutti. That was very difficult for me because they didn't know I was pregnant or that I was in Boston, Massachusetts trying to get married.

Their answer came in ten days. I was surprised it was so soon and that they gave me their okay. Since they couldn't write or speak English, my sister Monika had her teacher help fill out the paper. All they had to do was sign and send it back to me.

I was sad when the papers arrived because my father wouldn't be here to give me away. I would've loved a big hug and kiss on the cheek from him. I

Maria, Gypsy Princess

longed to feel his rough beard on my smooth face. Our love was so deep it didn't matter how far we were apart. It was etched in our hearts and would be there forever.

In the meantime, I sat alone in the room most of the time and didn't have any idea what would happen to me or if we would really get married. But I was also excited. I could hardly wait to tell Marvin we could get married now. I had to wait for his call to find out if he could get leave again that weekend.

Two days later he called to say he'd be off duty in a couple of days and had something important to talk to me about. He would not say what it was, and I didn't like the tone of his voice. A verboten feeling crept into my stomach, even as the baby started to kick.

I spent two bad days waiting for Marvin. When I saw his face when he entered the living room I could tell it was not good news. Without giving me a kiss he told me to sit down, and I knew I was in trouble. He started by saying he liked me, but he was still in love with his high school sweetheart he had known since kindergarten, and she had written him a long letter begging him not to marry me. He went on to say that he shouldn't marry someone he didn't really know and she also reminded him they had been waiting for each other for years, and had been careful not to make love until after they were married.

She was still waiting for him, and if he got leave she would marry him as soon as they could get a license. She went on and on about all the wonderful times they'd had over the years and did he really want to throw all that love and devotion away on a fling?

All this time I sat there not saying a word, and when he finished he looked at me with sad eyes, hoping I would not break into tears. I sat very still and my face must have been white as snow because he jumped up and got a glass of water and made me take a sip. When I revived a little, I still didn't respond. I didn't know what to say. I didn't know if I had heard him correctly, and wondered what he was planning to do now. Was he saying goodbye to me?

Did he want me to give him my blessing or cry and call him names? I didn't do anything. I was too shocked to move or cry. Crying wasn't my style. I had gone through too many unpleasant things in my life to cry in front of him. I would cry tomorrow when I was alone as I had done so many times in the past.

He was waiting for my answer, but what could I say? Don't leave me? What will I do now? I have nowhere to go?

I just waited for him to tell me his plans.

"I am sorry," he said, "but I don't love you and I don't want to get married. I want to marry my sweetheart from home. I've known her all my life and we made plans to get married some day and have a lot of kids. I just can't let her down. I love her with all my heart."

I asked him what he thought I should do now.

"Well, you'll just have to go back home to North Dakota ."

"How am I supposed to do get there?" I asked. "I have no money." The tears were now flowing freely and I had no more words.

"I'll figure it out," he said. "I have some back pay coming, and I can give you forty now to hold you over. The rent isn't due for two more weeks, and by then I'll get the money for your ticket home."

There was nothing more to say so he got up and gave me a little peck on the cheek. I stood there stunted, not able to move. He took some money out of his pocket, put it in my hand and walked out the door.

I don't know how long I stood there. I was in a daze and went and lay on the bed and cried. I must have fallen asleep because when I awoke it was dark outside, and I was hungry. I really didn't feel like eating but knew I had to eat for the baby's sake. Marvin had left the radio, and I turned it on made myself a sandwich and some tea. I ate and listened to the big band sounds and the music soothed my soul somewhat.

The next few days I walked around in a daze. I went downstairs to tell Helen what had happened. She was shocked.

"What will you do now?"

"I don't know. I don't have money to buy a ticket to North Dakota . I can't ask my folks for help. They don't have any money either. I'm waiting for Marvin to send me some. He promised to get enough together for the ticket and food to get me back home.

I wrote to my friend Melanie Werner, and she said I could come back and stay with them until the baby was born. That was very generous of her. Yes, she was a peach of a person, not only generous but sweet and beautiful too.

I sat in the apartment day after day. Waiting to hear from Marvin was getting me down and I really didn't know how to get a hold of him, so I just had to wait. After a week went by I got really worried. How would I pay the rent or get back home?

I was too big with child to get a job and I could not mooch off the Helen forever. She had been great, but enough was enough. Her boyfriend was asking her how long I could hold out without money coming in. She had no answer and neither did I.

Finally, only had a couple of days before I had to pay the rent, Helen took matters into her own hands and called social services. She explained my situation and they took charge and sent someone out to talk to me. I don't know if they got a hold of Marvin and the money came from him, but they bought my ticket to get back to Morehead , Minnesota . I sent a telegram to

Melanie telling her when I would arrive and also to my parents to let them know I wasn't getting married and was coming back to Morehead in a few days.

I was grateful to Helen and offered to baby-sit so she and her friend could have an evening out before I left. While they were out, I fell asleep on the sofa and didn't even hear them come home. They decided to leave me there and go to bed. When I woke I heard all kinds of noises coming from the bedroom. At first I was worried, but then I realized that they were having sex. So I went to my own bed upstairs.

A couple of days later the lady from social services came with a car and driver and drove me to the train station. She came along to make sure I got on the train all right and had everything I needed for the trip. The train ride was lonely and trying. I was uncomfortable being so big, which made for a long tiresome trip. I couldn't sleep much so I cried most of the way, and when I saw Melanie at the station I was so happy my eyes filled again with tears. I was so relieved to see her and to be back with a friend, someone I knew well and who cared what happened to me. It made me truly grateful, and I am still grateful she was in my life.

Chapter 21
Back in Moorhead, Minnesota

I was happy to get back to Moorhead. Melanie was a Godsend and helped me with everything. The only problem was I had to sleep with their youngest daughter Lorie, and she still wet the bed. So most mornings we both woke up all wet, but I had to sleep there until the baby was born.

It was now late January and very cold with a lot of snow outside, so I spent a lot of time in the house. It was a long cold one and a half months. I could hardly wait to get this child out of me. As all pregnant women know, the last two months are hardest, and I was getting very emotional and weepy, along with being big as a house.

I had no idea what to do after the baby was born. My folks wrote that I could bring him or her home to live with them until I knew what I wanted to do. I was grateful. I hadn't asked them for any help because I knew they had their own problems. They had recently moved to the town of Driscoll , and for the time being they and had to pay rent, which was a hardship because they had very little money. Since they had bought some farmland and were now in the process of acquiring a house to put on their property, they had their hands full. They couldn't move the house from Driscoll until the weather was nicer. Also the ground had to thaw so they could dig a basement then set the house on it.

My son David Scott Reule was born February 25, 1953, in Moorhead , Minnesota twelve days before my 18th Birthday.

Maria, Gypsy Princess

Maria at eighteen

My water broke in the middle of the night and at first I thought Lorie had wet the bed again, but when I started to have sharp pains I realized the baby wanted to come out now. I must have screamed, and Melanie and her husband Bruce woke and came running. She took over. She removed my night gown and helped me put my clothes on, then drove me to St. Agnes hospital. I was put on a stretcher and rushed into a room. Nurses came and asked me questions, then shaved my pubic hair and gave me an enema. The enema hurt more than the labor pains.

When the enema started to work I sat on the toilet, and I thought the baby was surely going to fall into the water and drown. I called the nurse to help me because I hurt so badly and I kept telling her my fears for the baby.

She assured me the baby wasn't ready to come out yet, the pains had to be closer together before I was ready to deliver. I didn't believe her and told her I didn't want my baby to fall into the water, so she stayed with me until I finished, then took me back and made me lie on the stretcher again. They took me into the delivery room and gave me some ether. I don't remember anything after that because when I woke up, I was lying in a bed with a drape around me. Melanie was sitting next to me, asking how I was feeling.

I was under ether so I answered, "I'm fine, but my baby is thirsty. Please give me some water."

She said, "I can't give you any water because of the ether. You'll get sick and throw up."

"Oh! You are mean. You won't even give my baby something to drink," I said, and she just looked at me and smiled. Just then the nurse came in and brought my baby and laid him in my arms. I took one look at the baby and said, "Oh, you poor thing who has been beating you up? Look at you, you're all black and blue and so red. You must have been in a fight. You poor, poor baby! Don't you worry I love you anyway." That said, I cuddled the baby close to me. I then laid him next to me and started to hum a German melody.

("Schlaf Kindlein, Schlaf, Dein Vater Hut die Schaf, dein Mutter hut die Lamerlein, Schlaf mein Kindlein Schlaf nur ein!")

When the nurse came back, I asked her, "What is it, a boy or a girl?"

"Why it's a boy, of course. Here, I'll show you. The nurse unfolded the blanket and when I bent down to look, he peed right in my face.

"Oh you little…" I started, then laughed and cuddled him to me. Melanie and the nurse bent over with laughter too.

I slept babbling all kinds of nonsense. Melanie told me she had to be going, but would be back the next day if she could.

"I'll see you in two days to pick you up, okay."

I said, "You're mean, to your children, because you won't give them any water to drink. Now you're leaving them and they have to fend for themselves again." With that I turned away and listened for the clip, clap of her shoes as she walked out of the room.

She did come the next evening when her husband could stay with the kids. This time I was nicer because the ether had worn off. I was in the hospital for three days. They gave me some pills to dry up my milk because I couldn't nurse the baby. I had to find a job as soon as I was able.

I stayed with the Werner's a few more days, then my brother Kurt, who called himself Jack now, came to pick me up and take me to our folk's place in Driscoll. In the car, Jack gave me a good talking to and asked how I could be so stupid and get myself pregnant, also why I hadn't told anyone.

I said, "I didn't get myself pregnant. It was done to me without my permission. I couldn't do anything about." I also told him I tried to give the baby away but I just couldn't. "So you better stop hounding me," I said, "I'm tired and I've had enough. I have gone through hell and back in the last nine months and I can do without your input. I already know what you're telling me. Leave me at peace, please, and just get me home because I don't feel too well."

"You're not going to throw up, are you?"

"No, I just had a baby, as you remember, and I'm sore all over. Please stop the car so I can get in the backseat to change and feed him." I got out and lay David on the back seat and changed him, then gave him his bottle. He slept the rest of the way home.

They must've been waiting and listening for the car to drive up, because as soon as it stopped the front door flew open and Mutti ran out. I opened the car door and couldn't even get out before she took David from me and started cooing over him. I got out, looked towards the house and saw Vati standing in the doorway frowning at me. I was worried. What if he was disappointed in me? I gave him a shy smile and walked toward him. That's when he smiled back. I was so happy to see his smile, I ran to him and put my arms around him, and he held me close. We stood there like that not saying a word.

There was a lot of commotion when we walked in, Moni and Mutti cooing and awing over the baby. I was grateful to all three of them for showing such love for my son.I knew he would be well cared for.I was happy to see Vati looked at David just as if he were his own son. I told Mutti he needed to be changed. She took charge and went into the bedroom to change him herself. I followed with the diaper bag and watched her fussing over him. She asked me in German if he was hungry and I answered in German that I'd fed him only a half hour ago and he didn't need t be fed for awhile. We laid him on the bed and put pillows around him in case he rolled over. I knew he wasn't old enough for that, but it made me more comfortable.

That afternoon I got really sick. I had a fever and was delirious. I lay on the sofa and dozed off. My folks were worried about me and didn't know what to do or why I had a fever. Later that day all I wanted was to be left alone or die, but instead the neighbors decided to visit and coo over the baby. I think they just wanted some thing to gossip about.

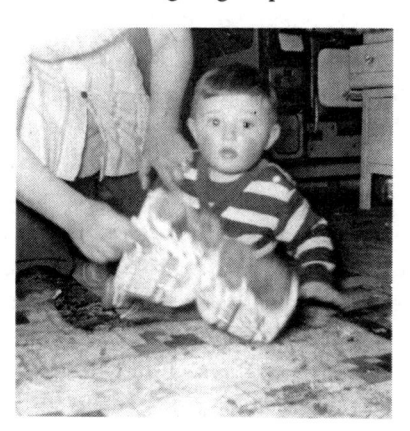

David a year old

    I tried to talk to them, but I was out of it and didn't know what I was saying.

    "Are you nursing the baby?" one of the women said. At first I didn't understand but she said, "Are you breast feeding David?"

    "No I bottle feed him?"

    "Did the doctor give you some pills?"

"Why, yes he did. Let's see, what did I do with them? Oh, I left them in Moorhead on the window sill."

"Maria, that's why you're sick, you have milk fever and you have to be careful because it could get serous. You'd better go to bed and drink a lot of liquids."

I didn't hear any more because I passed out cold.

When I awoke later I had a cold towel on my forehead, and it was dusk outside. Jack had left before I got sick or he would've gone for a doctor. He had to get back to Jamestown to put his affairs in order because he had been inducted into the American army and in two weeks he had to report for boot camp.

When he left he said he'd be back in a few days to take me to Jamestown with him. Yes, I was going back to the same town where it all began when I came to America.

I was really sick and in and out of consciousness all evening and through the night. Thank God, the next day I felt better. I stayed at home for a week until I felt well enough to travel. I also wanted to make sure David was settled in. The second day he started to fuss and cry a lot. He became colicky because his formula didn't agree with him, and we didn't know what to do. Mutti came up with a solution. She sent Monika to get some fresh cow milk. Mutti boiled it and after it cooled, she skimmed it and put it in the bottle, and after that he was happy and quiet as a lamb.

I hated to leave him. I hadn't even gotten to know him yet. I didn't have a photo of him either and would miss him. We didn't have a camera. I hoped someone in Driscoll would take a picture of us, but no such luck. To this day I don't have a photo of David as a baby. The first picture I have of him was on his first birthday. Vati and Mutti wanted to keep David and adopt him, but I wasn't sure I was ready for that. I asked if they would just please take care of him until I got on my feet. I would be forever grateful. I was sad to leave David behind and go to work, so I left a little note saying, "Mama loves you, David. See you soon."

Maria, Gypsy Princess

David on the farm

David, Mutti and Vati

"Good old Mrs. Mack gave me a job at the Moline Café again, a great lady, she never let me down." I was now eighteen years old and had more experience than most people have in a lifetime. I didn't know what lay in my future, but I was positive I could handle whatever life threw at me. I also knew life isn't fair sometimes and I might endure more hardships in the future, but with God's help I'd do all right and would live my life to the fullest.

Epilogue

I should explain about Marvin and P.J. Kruger. When I went to marry Marvin in Boston I really didn't realize Marvin wasn't the father. Maybe because I wanted Marvin to be David's father. He was the first real boyfriend I had.

I had put the incident with P.J. Kruger out of my mind. I also didn't think I could get pregnant in one encounter. At seventeen that's how naive I was, or ignorant because no one ever told me anything. When I was little and for a long time I thought babies where brought by storks. Of course, I knew better by then, but I didn't even notice I had stopped having my period until Mrs. Mack asked me about it.

It didn't dawn on me that P.J. was the baby's father until after David was born. It was when my brother Jack and I were driving from Driscoll to Jamestown . I was dozing in the front seat and thinking of my son when suddenly I realized my son's coloring was wrong for Marvin to be his father. Marvin was blond and blue eyed and David had black hair and dark black eyes just like P.J. Kruger.

Marvin never contacted me to offer support for the baby, so he never found out if I had a boy or a girl or that David wasn't his.

I saw P. J. Kruger again in October 1953. I ran into him when I was walking out of the Moline Café and he was coming in.

He stopped. "Hi Maria," he said, "long time no see."

I looked up, not recognizing him at first.

"Oh, it's you. Ja, not long enough," I said. "I have to tell you something, but not here. Can we go somewhere and talk?"

"Sure, let's go get a burger."

"Okay," I said, reluctantly.

His car was parked at the corner so we got in and took off.

We made small talk while we ate and then he asked me what I wanted to talk about.

I looked around the crowded restaurant. "I'll tell you on the way home."

In the car he tried to give me a kiss. I pushed him away and told him to drive. I didn't quite know how to begin, so I just blurted it out.

"P.J., you have a son named David. He's living with my folks in Driscoll." I expected him to be shocked, but he didn't even flinch. Instead he had that same smirk I remembered from our "date."

"Well, isn't that nice," he said. "I always wanted a son. How old is he?"

"You should know. Figure it out. He was born February 25th. He's eight months."

"Why didn't you tell me about him before? Are you sure he's mine?"

"Yes, I'm sure." I kept my voice low, but I could taste the anger.

"I was a virgin when you forced yourself on me, remember?"

"Sure, you said so, but how do I know it was true?"

"Well, do you want to take a blood test?" I asked.

"No, I believe you. But I wish you'd told me right away. If you'd said something we'd be married by now."

I stared at him. "Married, you must be kidding! I wouldn't marry you if you were the last human on earth. You're cruel. I'd rather live in hell than with you."

"Oh come on, we'll go get a marriage license tomorrow. We can tie the knot this weekend." He gave me a nudge. "Then we'll be mama and papa to little David."

I could not believe him, as if it was all a game. "You're crazy! After what you did to me?"

"Here I am willing to make you my wife and be David's father, but you make a big deal out of what happened last year. The past is gone, let's start over."

"You make it sound easy. You have no idea what I went through. You're a mean son of bitch, hardly marriage material."

"Maria, let's seal it with a kiss."

He leaned closer, but I pulled back. "No, you don't. Take me home. Now."

"Sure, but first I'll take you to meet my mother. I know she'll love you like I do."

He was mocking me. "Love! It was my first time and you forced me. You made it ugly. You spoiled my life, everything is ruined now."

"Hey, I'm willing to marry you." He shrugged. "You're the one who keeps saying no."

"Take me home. I just wanted you to know you have a son, in case you want to see him or do something for him." For a moment he didn't answer. "Well, say something!"

His voice changed. "All I want is to marry you and be a family. If you don't want to marry me, you can go to the devil."

"Fine." I opened the door. I would walk home. What I should've done that night. He grabbed my wrist and tried to kiss me, his other hand on my breast. But this time I was too quick for him. I twisted out of his grip, got out and ran down the street. I heard him shouting after me.

"Okay, walk home. See if I care. You'll never see or hear from me again."

I ran all the way, afraid he might follow and grab me again. I made it home and went right to bed, thankful to be finished with him.

That was the end of P.J. Kruger in my life. We never crossed paths again. I never found out his actual first name and have no idea what happened to him. David never knew his father and didn't ask me about him until many years later. That's when I told him this story.

As I wrote at the beginning, God has a purpose for us all. We are here on this earth to learn lessons from life, and perhaps we come back to do it over and over until we get it right. I always had this strong feeling I was a princess in a previous life and lived in luxury, and this time around I experienced the other side of the coin. So I could know the ugliness, violence and greed of mankind.

It doesn't end. It only goes a different direction. I was now a mother, my life changed forever. A new story was just beginning and there would be a lot more to tell, and God willing life would eventually be easier and full of love. I found happiness raising my baby boy, and I knew I would find more happiness before the end.

Since I am in my sixties now, I can tell you my life hasn't been a piece of cake, but I came through and am alive to tell about it. This story is just the first part of my life. There are many more years to tell.

****

I did make it to California.

It was now 1976. My husband, Robert Woelfl, (Bob) was my prince and we lived in Indian Wells, California. I had a cleaning lady now who came every other week.

On a Friday afternoon, June 29, 1976, Bob and I were getting ready to go play twilight golf, the last round of the tournament. The doorbell rang and Bob answered it. It was a telegram from my sister, Monica. I knew it was bad news even before he opened it.

VATI DIED JUNE 28 STOP HEART ATTACK STOP FUNERAL IS MONDAY STOP LET US KNOW IF YOU ARE COMING STOP LOVE MUTTI.

Father at eighty-two

I got dizzy, and my legs went weak, but Bob caught me in his arms.

Oh, God, not Vati, I thought. We had planned to visit them in August.

They lived in West Palm Beach now, with Monica, and her husband, Ray. Monica and Ray had a son, Chris, and a daughter, Lisa Marie, from Monica's first marriage. Jack and Helga lived in Miami. I was glad Mutti was surrounded by her children.

Bob held me for a long time. "Honey, are you alright?" he said finally. "You know we really should go. "It won't do you any good sitting around here crying. Please come. You can't get a flight out until tomorrow. It's best to take your mind off your loss."

I don't remember much of the game. After we finished and had dinner, we gave out the prizes to the winners. One of our friends went up to the mike and honored us for running the twilight tournament for three months. They surprised us with a lovely figurine of a swan. When we went up to receive the gift I had tears in my eyes. They all thought it was because of their generosity, but my tears were for my father.

I arrived in West Palm Beach the next day. Jack and Helga picked me up from the airport. Jack hugged me. "Hi, sis, glad to see you." Helga just waved from the car. At the house, Mutti fell into my arms crying. We hugged each other for several minutes. Moni finally pulled us into the house and gave me a hug.

(Mutti and I had become good friends over the years. I was the link between the old and the new family. Many a times Mutti would call my asking me for help, for insight into my fathers heart and mind. "I knew him so well."

We shared "His" love.

I hadn't met three-year-old Chris yet, and he wanted his mama's attention. Later I went and sat with Mutti to talk. We were both crying. I tried to comfort her, but needed comforting myself. All I wanted was to curl up in a corner and be left alone to cry. The next day we were to go to the chapel where Vati would be laid out. They decided to have an open casket. I didn't agree. I wanted to remember Father as he was, happy, a smile on his face and a song in his heart. I wanted to hear again the German songs he used to sing to us and the fairy tales he told us at bedtime.

I didn't want to see him lying there with his beautiful brown eyes closed. I was out voted and the casket stayed open. They had made the arrangements without asking me. I didn't want to make problems, so I let it go.

When it was time for the viewing I went for Mutti. The chapel was tastefully done, flowers and candles everywhere. I sat in back and cried quietly while everyone went up to the casket. Jack came and tried to coax me to come forward and say farewell to Vati. I told him no, I would rather remember Father as he had been. He took my hands, lifted me from my chair and practically pushed me to the front of the chapel. Again I didn't want to make a scene so I looked at my dead father lying in the casket. I wish I hadn't. He looked peaceful, but he was not my Papa.

I dreamed of him that night. In my dream he was no longer my father, but a death mask coming towards me. I woke shaking. The funeral seemed to have nothing to do with me. The minister didn't even know who I was and tried to seat me in the second row. I insisted on sitting in front with Helga and Jack. He was my father, not theirs. Monica apparently only told the minister about her mother's side of the family. The obituary in the local paper didn't even include my name or any of Father's children from his first marriage. It was too late to do anything about it.

Afterwards at the house we took family photos on the front steps. I just wanted to be left alone. I didn't want to talk to anyone. I lay on the sofa in the family room out of the way. Then Chris came in and started pulling on me. "My place," he said. "Get up. My place." Monica told him to leave Aunt Maria alone, but he started to cry repeating, "My place. My place."

I got up and went to Mutti's and Vati's apartment over the garage and lay on the sofa there. Jack came and sat next to me. He was drunk. I thought he was there to comfort me, but instead he became hostile, ranting about how he was Vati's favorite. That he had done everything for Mutti and Vati when they lived on the farm, and all I ever did was bring David home for them to take care of. "I just wanted you to know Vati loved me most," he slurred.

I looked at him through my tears, stunned eyes stunt that he was so cruel. I wanted to tell him he didn't know what he was talking about. He wasn't there when I was little. He had no idea how close Vati and I were. He was jealous because Vati wasn't his father. He was mean, miserable and bitter so he kept sputtering, and saying cruel things to me. He said, "I have always been helpful to Vati and Mutti and you were a disappointment to them." He went on and on, while I cried.

Finally Helga came into the room and shooed Jack out.

I told her what he had said.

"Oh, Maria, don't listen to him, he's just drunk and he gets crazy when he drinks."

"He has no right to talk to me like that," I said, "especially now."

I went into the other room and closed the door laid down and stayed there all night.

The next day Mutti wondered why I wouldn't talk to Jack. I didn't want to tell her so I told her to ask Jack. Later I was helping Monica in the kitchen and she could tell I was upset and asked why. I told her what Jack said the night before.

"We all know how much Vati loved you," she said. "You were his favorite. Anyone could tell. Whenever he talked about you his eyes would light up. He truly loved you. His gypsy princess."

I smiled knowing his love would be with me through eternity.

Maria Reule Woelfl

Maria in her Wedding Gown"

Bob & Maria's, wedding

Maria, Gypsy Princess

Father gave me away